Men, Women, and the Mystery of Love

Practical Insights from
John Paul II's
Love and Responsibility

• Edward Sri •

servant

AN IMPRINT OF
FRANCISCAN MEDIA
Cincinnati, Ohio

ALSO BY EDWARD SRI

The Advent of Christ:
Scripture Reflections to Prepare for Christmas

Dawn of the Messiah:
The Coming of Christ in Scripture

The New Rosary in Scripture:
Biblical Insights for Praying the 20 Mysteries

Cover and book design by Mark Sullivan

LIBRARY OF CONGRESS CATALOGING-IN-PUBLICATION DATA
(from original edition)
Sri, Edward P.
Men, women, and the mystery of love : practical insights from John Paul II's Love and responsibility / by Edward Sri.
p. cm.
Includes bibliographical references.
ISBN 978-0-86716-840-2 (pbk. : alk. paper) 1. John Paul II, Pope, 1920-2005. Milosc i odpowiedzialnosc. 2. Sex—Religious aspects—Catholic Church. 3. Sexual ethics. 4. Catholic Church—Doctrines. I. Title.
BT708.S666 2007
241'.66—dc222007016657

ISBN 978-1-63253-080-6

Published by Servant, an imprint of Franciscan Media
28 W. Liberty St.
Cincinnati, OH 45202
www.FranciscanMedia.org

Printed in the United States of America.
Printed on acid-free paper.
15 16 17 18 19 5 4 3 2 1

. . . .

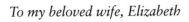

To my beloved wife, Elizabeth

contents

I am grateful to the many young adults, married couples, and religious who have explored John Paul II's *Love and Responsibility* with me throughout the years, especially my students at the Augustine Institute, students at Benedictine College, the missionaries and students in FOCUS (Fellowship of Catholic University Students), and the sisters in the Eastern Region of the Missionaries of Charity.

I am also grateful to Kirsten Goza for her thoughtful reflection questions, many of which are found at the end of each chapter. Particular thanks goes to Leon Suprenant, Mike Sullivan, and the staff at *Lay Witness* magazine who invited me to write about *Love and Responsibility* in 2005–2006. Their encouragement and feedback was tremendously helpful for my pursuit of this topic, and those original articles served as the groundwork for this present book.

I also express thanks to the many Augustine Institute students, FOCUS missionaries, and individuals from around the world who have shared their stories with me about how the insights from John Paul II discussed in this book have impacted their lives: their friendships, their dating relationships, and their marriages. Some of the common themes and stories from this feedback throughout the years have been included in the new edition of this book. Special thanks goes to Louise Pare and the team at Servant who encouraged me to pursue this new edition and worked tirelessly to make it possible.

My deepest gratitude is for my wife, Elizabeth—for her loving support throughout this project and the ways she strives to live "Love and Responsibility" in our own marriage.

"This is dangerous. Don't let my wife see this!"

That's how a friend of mine jokingly responded when he first came across the challenging insights on love, marriage, and male-female relationships in St. John Paul II's book *Love and Responsibility*. Indeed, I know of no other book that so brilliantly sheds light on the mysterious dynamics between men and women and at the same time so poignantly challenges us to live out those relationships better—as *Love and Responsibility*.

Written in the late 1950s in Eastern bloc, Soviet-dominated Poland, *Love and Responsibility* prophetically anticipated many of the needs our own post-sexual-revolutionized Western world would face decades later. In an era like ours, when there is much confusion about love and marriage and when many people are struggling in their relationships with the opposite sex, John Paul II's insights from *Love and Responsibility* are perhaps needed now more than ever before.

But beware: *Love and Responsibility* is truly life transforming. John Paul II's vision for love is so captivating that it may change the way you think about love, friendship, and relationships as a whole. If taken to heart, the wisdom from *Love and Responsibility* will change the way you interact with the opposite sex. It will change the way you date. It will change the way you relate to your spouse. It will make you a better husband or wife.

Some of the very practical, real-life relationship issues that *Love and Responsibility* addresses include:

- *Friendship:* What makes a true friendship and how this kind of friendship lays the foundation for love.
- *Attraction:* The two main ways men and women are attracted to each other and how these attractions can lead either to friendship and selfless love or to a relationship in which someone is being used.
- *Relationships:* How do I know if I am in a relationship of authentic love or just another relationship that is doomed to failure? Why don't some relationships pass the test of time? What ingredients are necessary for true love?
- *Men and Women:* The differences between men and women and the particular needs of a man and a woman in marriage.
- *Love:* The two aspects of love and how knowing the difference is crucial for any relationship with the opposite sex.
- *The Emotions:* The difference between *feeling* "I'm in love" and love itself. How the emotions can either be incorporated into love or hinder true love from ever developing.
- *Sexuality:* Why should people wait until they are married to have sex? What constitutes a lustful thought? The problem of pornography. How is human sexual desire different from animal instinct?
- *Marriage:* How can I build greater trust and intimacy in my marriage? How do I deal with my beloved's faults? How can I be a better spouse? How can I grow in self-giving love?
- *Chastity:* How to win the fight for purity in our relationships and in our hearts.

As one can see, *Love and Responsibility* is not a dry manual on sexual ethics or an abstract treatise on love. When read properly, it is down-to-earth and sheds much light on the real issues we face in our relationships with the opposite sex. Furthermore, *Love and Responsibility* is not just about marriage. More broadly, it delves into the dynamics of love between men and women at all stages of relationships, whether it be friendship, dating, engagement, or married life.

My own writing on *Love and Responsibility* flows out of my teaching on this book for people of various ages and states of life. While much attention has been given to John Paul II's later work on love and sexuality known as the Theology of the Body, *Love and Responsibility* is not as well known. Yet I have

"This is dangerous. Don't let my wife see this!"

been impressed at how virtually everyone—college students and young adults, engaged couples and married couples, priests and religious—finds John Paul II's insights from *Love and Responsibility* extremely useful and immediately applicable to their own lives and relationships. As one marriage counselor told me, "Theology of the Body is fascinating, but *Love & Responsibility* changes the way you treat your spouse on Monday morning."

Along this line, I intend this guide through *Love and Responsibility* to be very practical—helping readers understand John Paul II's vision for relationships between men and women and then make application to their own lives. This is not an academic analysis or a comprehensive treatment of *Love and Responsibility*. Rather, I simply aim to make some of the insights from this challenging philosophical work more accessible to the average lay reader and offer some of my own reflections along the way.

I also do not intend this book to be an exhaustive relationship manual, answering all questions about relationships with the opposite sex. In fact, sometimes these reflections will raise even more questions than they answer. This is to be expected. John Paul II himself does not offer a specific road map for every relationship issue and situation. He does, however, offer us general principles that we can apply to our own particular circumstances.

On an even more basic level, simply getting us to think about these issues more closely and raise questions that we've not considered before can serve a great good. For if these insights from *Love and Responsibility* get us to examine more closely our own hearts and how we approach our relationships with the opposite sex, we may be more likely to avoid the many relational pitfalls that can easily trap us. At the same time, these insights can inspire us to live out our relationships with greater Christlike love.

This book is made for a variety of situations: small-group study, marriage preparation classes and other parish settings, or individual personal reading. And it is made for a wide range of people—young adults, engaged couples, newlyweds, single people, people married for thirty years, and even priests and religious. Each chapter includes some reflection questions that can be used either for group discussion or personal consideration. Each chapter also includes recommendations for further reading in *Love and Responsibility* itself for those who would like to follow along in John Paul II's work as they read the reflections in this book. Quotations are taken from the H.T. Willets translation of *Love and Responsibility* (San Francisco: Ignatius, 1993) with page numbers from this edition included in parentheses.

This updated release of *Men, Women, and the Mystery of Love* contains all the material from the original edition, but also includes new reflections and stories from young people and married couples who have shared with me over the years how the ideas discussed in this book have had an impact on their lives. Their personal examples shed additional light on how *Love and Responsibility* can be applied to men-women relationships, and you will find these new insights sprinkled in at different points throughout this book.

This new edition also offers two new chapters: one that describes how John Paul II's wisdom can be lived out in singlehood in a way that forms readers for a strong marriage or for whatever state in life God may be calling them to, plus a chapter written for engaged couples on how to apply *Love and Responsibility* to their marriage preparation.

It is my hope that the reflections in this book will help all readers benefit from John Paul II's vision for love and sexuality and find great relevance for their own lives.

chapter one

The Three Kinds of Friendship

What can a celibate priest really teach us about love, sexuality, and relationships between men and women?

That's the question a Polish priest, Father Karol Wojtyla, addressed in the introduction to his revolutionary book *Love and Responsibility*. Published in 1960, this book on sexual ethics was the fruit of Wojtyla's extensive pastoral work with young people and his philosophical reflections on this topic while serving as a priest and university professor in Krakow—long before the world would come to know him as Pope John Paul II.

In *Love and Responsibility*, Wojtyla argues that while a priest may lack direct experience in marriage and sexuality, he has something that gives him an even wider perspective on these matters: a broad secondhand experience. As a spiritual adviser who worked closely with many young adults and married couples amid their struggles in love and sexuality, Father Wojtyla was able to draw from the experiences of a wide range of personalities, relationships, and marriages in a way that the individual average layman could not. *Love and Responsibility* is the fruit of this rich pastoral experience as well as his own philosophical and theological reflection on love, sex, and marriage.

A "Great Book"

Janet Smith, one of the leading teachers in America on Catholic sexual ethics, argues that *Love and Responsibility* is not just an important book, but that it should be recognized in the lists of the greatest works of Western civilization. Right up there with Homer's *Iliad*, Dante's *Divine Comedy,* and Augustine's *Confessions,* we should expect to find John Paul II's *Love and Responsibility* among the great books read for centuries to come. She says, "I maintain that the Pope's book belongs in this group, since I think generations to come will read his book—they certainly should do so, for if they do they will find that it boldly confronts questions we all have about life and offers a way of viewing human relationships which, if accepted, would radically alter the way in which we conduct our lives."[1]

Indeed, *Love and Responsibility*'s insights on male-female relationships are truly life transforming and desperately needed today. Growing up in the aftermath of the sexual revolution, the younger generation especially is hungering for any wise guidance they can get on how to navigate their relationships with the opposite sex. Single people, engaged couples, and married spouses all will find in *Love and Responsibility* not only a very different perspective from what the world offers, but a view that, once encountered, cannot help but have a positive impact on the way they relate to one another.

Putting the Person First

John Paul II's first major task in *Love and Responsibility* is to lay out what he calls the personalist principle. According to this foundational principle for human relationships, "...a person must not be *merely* the means to an end for another person" (26). In other words, we should never treat the people in our lives as mere instruments for achieving our own purposes.

He explains why this is so. Human persons have free will and are capable of self-determination. Unlike the animals that act according to their instincts and appetites, persons can use their reason and act deliberately. Through self-reflection, persons can choose a course of action for themselves and assert their "inner self" to the outside world through their choices.

Thus, each person is utterly unique. No one else can think for me. No one else can choose for me. To treat another human person merely as an instrument for my own purposes is to violate the dignity of the person as a self-determining being. "This being so, every person is by nature capable of determining his or her aims. Anyone who treats a person as the means to an end does violence to the very essence of the other, to what constitutes its natural right" (27).

Utilitarianism

What makes it difficult to live out this basic principle for human relationships is the spirit of utilitarianism that pervades our society. In this view, the best human actions are those that are most useful. And something is useful in so far as it maximizes pleasure and comfort for me and minimizes pain and discomfort. The underlying assumption is that happiness consists in pleasure. Therefore, I should always pursue whatever brings me comfort, advantage, and benefit and avoid whatever may cause me suffering, disadvantage, and loss.

This utilitarian view affects the way we relate to one another. If my main goal in life is to pursue my own pleasure, then I weigh my choices in life in light of how much they lead me to this goal. Utilitarianism is so much a part of the modern world that many people today—even good Christians—may approach a relationship in terms of how useful a person is in helping them achieve their goals or how much fun they have with this person.

Here's a scenario many young people say they find themselves in that illustrates this point. It's Tuesday and a friend asks you if you have plans for Friday night. You're free, so you say, "No, I don't have anything going on that night." What do you do when your friend invites you to go with him and others to a fun party? Are you likely to say yes to your friend right away? Many young people say they tend to delay committing themselves to their friend's invitation and instead say something like, "Hmmm. Maybe.... We'll have to see.... Can I get back to you later in the week?"

> "I'm not sure I've ever had real friends. There were just people around me."

Why do many of us (not just young people) do that? If we're free on Friday night and a friend invites us to do something that we'd like to do, why don't we just say, "Yes, thank you for the invitation. I'd love to go with you to that party"? As many college students and young adults have admitted to me, often the main reason we don't commit to our friends in a situation like this is because we want to keep our options open in case someone else plans an even more exciting social event for Friday night, or in case that particular guy or gal we're interested in wants to do something with us that evening. We don't commit to the invitation right in front of us so we can be available should something more enjoyable come our way later.

If that's the case, then why don't we just say no to our friend's invitation? Sometimes we're afraid of hurting the other person's feelings. Yet as many young people admit, there's often another motive. We frequently go with the "maybe" response and avoid giving a definitive "no" because we don't want to close the door *completely* on this particular option. If nothing better comes up for Friday night, we want to have this possibility still available. In other words, we want to keep this friend as a backup. This is just one example from everyday life illustrating how much utilitarianism affects the way many of us view our friendships.

LOVING OR USING?

This outlook is dangerous. John Paul II says that once these utilitarian attitudes are adopted, we begin to reduce the people in our lives to objects to use for our own enjoyment (37).

This helps explain why many friendships, dating relationships, and even marriages today are so fragile and so easily dissolved. If I value a woman only insofar as she is advantageous for me to know or only to the extent that I derive some pleasure from being with her, then there is not much of a foundation for the relationship. As soon as I cease to experience pleasure or benefit from my time with her—or as soon as I can find more pleasure or benefit with someone else—she no longer is valuable to me. This view is quite far from the personalist principle and even farther from a relationship of committed love.

THREE KINDS OF FRIENDSHIP

It may be helpful at this point to mention the different kinds of friendship as described by Aristotle, whom John Paul II cites in his discussion of love.[2]

According to Aristotle, there are three kinds of friendship based on three kinds of affection that unite people. First, in a *friendship of utility*, the affection is based on the benefit or use the friends derive from the relationship. Each person gets something out of the friendship that is to his advantage, and the mutual benefit of the relationship is what unites the two people as friends.

Many work-related friendships fall under this category. Let's say Bob owns a construction company in Boston. He has a friendship with Sam in San Francisco because Sam sells the kind of nails that Bob needs, at the best price. For their business exchanges, Bob and Sam see each other a few times a year, talk on the phone about once a week, and e-mail each other regularly. Over the years of doing business together, they have learned about each other's careers, families, and interests. They get along well and sincerely wish each other all the best in life. They are friends, but what unites them is the particular benefit they each receive from the friendship: nails for Bob and sales for Sam.

Second, in a *pleasant friendship*, the basis of affection is the pleasure one gets out of the relationship. One sees the friend as a cause of some pleasure for himself. This friendship is primarily about having fun together. The friends may listen to the same music, play the same sport, enjoy the same form of exercise, live in the same dormitory, or hang out at the same nightclub. The two people may sincerely care about each other and wish each other well in life, but what unites them as friends is primarily the good times they experience together.

FRAGILE FOUNDATIONS

Aristotle notes that while useful and pleasant friendships are basic forms of friendship, they do not represent friendship in the fullest sense. Useful and pleasant friendships are the most fragile. They are the least likely to stand the test of time because when the mutual benefits or fun times no longer exist, there is nothing left to unite the two people. For example, if Sam leaves the nail selling business to sell books, what will happen to his friendship with Bob now that he no longer sells nails? Sam and Bob may still exchange Christmas cards and e-mail every once in a while, but since they no longer need to communicate regularly for their business transactions, their friendship most likely will begin to dissolve. The relationship is no longer mutually useful.

Similarly, in the pleasant friendship, when one person's interests change or one's friend moves away and is no longer around to share good times, the friendship is likely to fade. This helps explain why friendships among young people shift so often. As they move from high school to college to the professional world, they mature, and their interests, values, moral convictions, and geographical locations change. If their friendships in these transitional years are not based on something more profound than the fact that they happened to live in the same dorm or play the same sport or have fun together, their friendships are likely to dissolve over time. Such friendships based on having good times together are unlikely to continue when one friend is no longer able to share those pleasurable experiences.

Sadly, many people today are very lonely. They never experience friendships that rise above utility or pleasure—that rise above sports, beer, gossip, the office, or hanging out. Many never really have friends with whom they can share what's deepest on their hearts and what matters most in life. As one young adult expressed, reflecting on the people he hung out with in the past, "The only reason I was friends with those people is that we'd go out, drink, and watch sports. We never really talked. We just didn't want to go out alone. But two years later I'm not in touch with any one of them." Another young adult put it more starkly: "I'm not sure I've ever had real friends. There were just people around me."

Virtuous Friendship

For Aristotle, the third form of friendship is friendship in the fullest sense. It can be called virtuous friendship because the two friends are united not in self-interest but in the pursuit of a common goal: the good life, the moral life that is found in virtue.

The problem with useful and pleasant friendships is that the emphasis is on what *I* get out of the relationship. However, in the virtuous friendship, the two friends are committed to pursuing something outside themselves, something that goes beyond each of their own self-interests. And it is this higher good that unites them in friendship. Striving side by side toward the good life and encouraging one another in the virtues, true friends are primarily concerned not with what *they* get out of the friendship but with what is best for the friend and with pursuing the virtuous life with that friend.

What Makes or Breaks a Relationship

With this background in mind, John Paul II gives us the key that will prevent our relationships from falling into the self-centered waters of utilitarianism. He says *the only way two human persons can avoid using each other is to relate in pursuit of a common good*, as in the virtuous friendship. If the other person sees what is good for me and adopts it as a good for himself, "...a special bond is established between me and this other person: the bond of a *common good* and of a common aim" (28). This common aim *unites people internally*. When we don't live our relationships with this common good in mind, we inevitably will treat the other person as a means to an end, for some pleasure or use.

Especially in marriage, there is a temptation to be self-centered, to want our spouse and children to conform to our plans, schedules, and preferences. For example: When I come home from work, I may concentrate on what I want to do (eat, read the paper, watch a game on TV, check e-mail) rather than give attention to what my kids need (a bath, help cleaning up toys, time with their dad) or what my wife needs (help cleaning the kitchen, a break, a husband to talk to).

When the weekend approaches, I may focus on the things *I* want to do—house projects *I* want to get done, work *I* want to get caught up on, sporting events *I* want to watch, things *I* want to look at online—without giving priority to what my wife and children may need from me. When it comes to family finances, I may joyfully agree to spend money on things that are important to me but strongly resist my wife's desire to invest in something that may not benefit me directly even though it may be important for our family.

> "True friends are primarily concerned not with what *they* get out of the friendship but with what is best for the friend."

Pope John Paul II reminds us that true friendship, especially friendship in marriage, must be centered on the bond of a common aim. In Christian marriage, that common aim involves the union of the spouses, the spouses serving each other and helping each other grow in holiness, and the procreation and education of children.

Our own individual preferences and agendas should be subordinated to these higher goods. Husband and wife must be subordinate to each other and to the good of their children, working to prevent any selfish individualism from creeping into their marriage. As a team, husband and wife work toward this common aim and discern *together* how best to use their time, energy, and resources to achieve those common goals of marriage.

John Paul II explains that being united in this common good helps spouses ensure that one person is not being used or neglected by the other. "*When two different people consciously choose a common aim* puts them on a footing of equality, and precludes the possibility that one of them might be subordinated to the other" (28–29). This is so because both are equally "...subordinated to that good which constitutes their common end" (28–29).

Without this common end, our relationships inevitably will fall into some form of using the person for our own benefit or pleasure. In the next chapter, we will consider how crucial these foundational points from *Love and Responsibility* are for navigating the emotional and physical attractions we often experience when we encounter people of the opposite sex.

FOR FURTHER READING
Love and Responsibility, pp. 21–44

FOR DISCUSSION AND REFLECTION

1.   John Paul II devoted much of his pontificate to promoting the principles he developed in *Love and Responsibility* regarding the relationships between men and women. Janet Smith claims that these foundational principles could "radically alter the way in which we conduct our lives." Why do you think such a work could be so critical for our time and culture?

2.   In your own words, how would you explain Wojtyla's concept of the personalist principle?

3.   How have you noticed or even experienced the spirit of utilitarianism—using others for one's personal benefit and pleasure—in relationships? Based on the observation that this "using" of others may take different forms for men and

women, what are some of the specific ways you have seen men and women use each other?

4. This chapter focuses on the three kinds of friendships. How have your friendships changed over the years? Have you experienced a relationship that you thought was true friendship only to realize that the other person was not committed to you as a person and not truly seeking your best interests? How might the description of "useful" or "pleasant" friendships shed light on this?

5. Have you ever experienced a truly virtuous friendship? What made it different from other relationships that were useful or pleasant friendships?

6. How do we fall into utilitarianism in our relationships? In other words, what keeps us from true virtuous friendships with friends and family members?

7. For married people: What are some ways you tend to focus on your own preferences in the home instead of serving the needs of your spouse and children? What are some practical things you can do to relate with your spouse in pursuit of a common aim, rather than just a pursuit of what's important to you? How can you shift even more from an attitude of "What would I prefer?" to "What is best for my spouse and our family?"

chapter two

Beyond the Sexual Urge

*I*n our first reflection on John Paul II's *Love and Responsibility,* we considered the personalist principle, which says that we should not treat other persons merely as a means to an end. In particular, we saw how utilitarianism weakens our relationships by getting us to value people primarily in terms of some pleasure or benefit we receive from our relationships with them.

Yet the sophisticated utilitarian may argue that there is nothing wrong with two people "using" each other as long as they mutually consent and mutually receive some advantage from the relationship. In fact, some might say such a relationship, which brings together the egoism (self-interest) of the man and the egoism of the woman in a mutually beneficial way, actually is a relationship of love.

For example, what is wrong with Bill and Sally having sex outside of marriage if each person consents and each person derives some pleasure from it? In the sexual act, Bill's desire for pleasure harmonizes with Sally's desire for pleasure so the act does not appear to be selfish. They each give pleasure to each other and don't just seek it for themselves.

John Paul II points out one serious problem with such a relationship: "The moment they cease to match and to be of advantage to each other, nothing at all is left of the harmony. Love will be no more, in either of the persons or between them" (39).

Since this kind of relationship is still dependent on what *I* get out of others, it prevents me from truly being in communion with them and being committed to them as persons. I'm "committed" to the person only insofar as—and as long as—I receive pleasure or advantage from the relationship. In fact, John Paul II likens such relationships of mutual use to prostitution.

LIKE PROSTITUTION

Consider a businessman who has a relationship with a prostitute on a certain night every week. The man desires the sexual pleasure she can give him, and the woman desires the money he can give her. They each have self-serving aims that come together in the sexual act and benefit the other person. They each get what they want, and in the process, they meet the other person's desires.

The moment they cease to be mutually advantageous to one another, however, what will happen to this relationship? If a richer man can pay the prostitute more on that particular night of the week, she likely will leave the first businessman for the wealthier one. On the other hand, if the businessman no longer finds the prostitute pleasurable and meets a younger, more attractive prostitute, he likely will leave the first for the younger one.

This may seem like an extreme example, but how many male-female relationships today are not much better than this? How many relationships are based more on a mutual use than on a committed love and a true communion of persons? For example, how many young women have sex with a man for the emotional security of having a boyfriend or for fear that if they don't do this, the man may break up with them? How often does a man just want a good-looking woman to sleep with for the physical pleasure he may derive from the relationship? These are not relationships of authentic love that bring persons in communion with one another. These are simply more socially acceptable forms of mutual use—but still similar to prostitution.

INSECURITY, NOT LOVE

John Paul II notes how utilitarian relationships breed fear and insecurity in one or both of the persons. A warning sign that one might be in a utilitarian relationship is when one person is afraid to bring up difficult topics or is afraid to address problems in the relationship.

One reason many dating, engaged, or married couples never confront one another with difficulties is that deep down they know there is not much foundation for the relationship to stand on, just the mutual pleasure or benefit. One fears that if the relationship becomes challenging, demanding, or difficult for the other person, that person may leave. "I never brought up any problems in the relationship, anything that might cause tension, because if I did, I knew it would get hard, and then it would be over," one young adult admitted. In utilitarian relationships, the only way the relationship can survive is to cover up problems and pretend things aren't as bad as they really are.

> "I never brought up any problems in the relationship...because if I did, I knew it would be over."

> Therefore, love so understood is self-evidently merely a pretense which has to be carefully cultivated to keep the underlying reality hidden: the reality of egoism, and the greediest kind of egoism at that, exploiting another person to obtain for itself its own "maximum pleasure." (39)

Letting Yourself Be Used

The pope then shows how people in these kinds of relationships sometimes even allow themselves to be used by the other person in order to get what they want out of the relationship: "...each of the persons is mainly concerned with gratifying his or her own egoism, but at the same time consents to serve someone else's egoism, because this can provide the opportunity for such gratification—and just as long as it does so" (39).

In this case, the person willingly lowers himself to be used as a tool for the other person's selfish intentions. For example, a man may do or say things that he might not ordinarily do or say in order to flatter a woman so that he can get something from her. He might buy her flowers or take her out to dinner, but he does this more for the emotional or sexual pleasure he hopes to receive from her than for a pure, selfless desire to honor her.

Similarly, a woman may do things with a man sexually that she ordinarily wouldn't do in order to get something out of the man, whether it be a sense of intimacy, a feeling of being loved, or the security she finds in having a boyfriend. "If I start by giving him what he wants," one woman said, "then maybe he'll eventually love me as a person."

Another young woman described her relationship with her boyfriend this way: "I knew he was just using me, and I let him. I thought that if I [were to] go along with this for a while, then he would eventually change and come to love me." But these desperate approaches never lead to authentic love. They are just other forms of manipulation and using the other person. She gives him sexual pleasure so she can have the feeling of being loved.

As John Paul II explains, "...if I treat someone else as a means and a tool in relation to myself I cannot help regarding myself in the same light. We have here something like the opposite of the commandment to love" (39).

THE SEXUAL URGE

Sexuality is one of the main areas where we can fall into using other people. John Paul II thus spends time reflecting on the nature of the sexual urge.

First, he discusses how the sexual urge manifests itself in the tendency for human persons to seek the opposite sex. He says the sexual urge orients a man toward the physical and psychological characteristics of a woman—her body, her femininity—which are the very attributes that are most complementary to the man. And the woman, in turn, is oriented toward the physical and psychological attributes of a man—his body, his masculinity—as the properties that are naturally complementary to the woman. Hence, the sexual urge itself is experienced as a bodily (physical) and emotional (psychological) attraction to a person of the other sex.

Nevertheless, the sexual urge is not an attraction to the physical or psychological qualities of the opposite sex *in the abstract*. John Paul II emphasizes that these attributes only exist in a concrete human person. For example, no man is attracted to blonde or brunette in the abstract. He is attracted to a *woman*—a particular *person*—who may have blonde or brunette hair. A woman is not primarily attracted to masculinity as a theoretical concept, but she may be very attracted to a particular *man* who exhibits certain traditionally masculine traits, such as courage, decisiveness, strength, and chivalry.

The reason John Paul II emphasizes this point is that he wants to show how the sexual urge ultimately is directed toward *a human person.* Therefore, the sexual urge is not bad in itself. In fact, since it is meant to orient us toward another person, the sexual urge can provide a framework for authentic love to develop.

This is not to say that the sexual urge is to be equated with love itself. Love involves a lot more than the spontaneous, sensual, or emotional reactions that are produced by the sexual urge; authentic love requires acts of the will directed toward the good of the other person. Still, the pope says that the sexual urge can provide the raw material from which acts of love may arise—if it is guided by a great sense of responsibility for the other person.

> "I knew he was just using me, and I let him."

MORE THAN ANIMAL INSTINCT

It is important to note that the sexual urge in human persons is not the same as the sexual instinct found in animals. Animals act according to their instincts and appetites. Human persons, however, are not enslaved to their passions and desires. With intellect and free will, persons can choose a course of action based on self-reflection no matter what desires may be stirring within them. For example, a very hungry man may desire to eat a ham sandwich that is offered to him, but he can choose not to follow his desire because he generously wants someone else to have the sandwich or because he has committed to fast on that particular day. A person can rise above appetites for the sake of a higher goal.

A dog, however, cannot do that. What happens when you put a steak in front of a normal, hungry dog? Is the dog going to take a pass on that steak to let the other hungry canines in the neighborhood have a chance to eat it? Will the dog say to himself, "I better not eat that. It's a Friday in Lent"? Of course not. A hungry dog will devour the piece of meat that sits before him!

Similarly, John Paul II explains that in animals, the sexual instinct is a reflex mode of action, not dependent on conscious thought. A female cat in heat does not reflect on what is the best time, place, or circumstance for her to mate, and she does not ponder which male cat in the neighborhood would make the ideal partner. Cats simply act reflexively, according to their instincts.

Human persons, however, are not called to live like the animals. They do not have to be enslaved to what is stirring within them in the sexual sphere. In the end, the person is in control of the sexual urge—not the other way around. The person can choose how he or she wants to use it (50).

A man, for example, may experience a sexual attraction to a woman. He may sometimes even experience this attraction as something *happening* to him— something that begins to take place in his sensual or emotional life without any initiative on his part. That attraction, however, can and should be subordinated to his intellect and will. While a person may not always be responsible for what spontaneously happens to him in the arena of sexual attraction, he *is* responsible for what he decides to do in response to those interior stirrings (46–47).

> "If I start by giving him what he wants, then maybe he'll eventually love me as a person."

LOVING OR ENJOYING?

Remember, the sexual urge draws us to the physical and psychological attributes of a person of the opposite sex. But ultimately, it is meant to orient us toward another *person* who possesses those attributes—*not just the attributes themselves*. Manifestations of the sexual urge thus present us with a choice between loving the person and using them for their attributes.

Let's say Jim meets Mary at work and is quickly attracted to her good looks and charming personality. Jim can choose to rise above this initial sexual reaction and see in her more than just her body or her femininity. By looking beyond the physical and psychological qualities that give him pleasure, he has the possibility of seeing her as a person and responding to her with selfless acts of love.

On the other hand, Jim may experience sexual attraction and choose to dwell on the physical and psychological qualities that give him pleasure. By focusing on her good looks and her feminine charm—and the pleasure he derives from them—he is distracted from seeing Mary as she is and remains incapable of truly loving her as a person. He may be kind to her, but he is doing this, at least to some significant degree, so he may receive some sensual or emotional pleasure from his association with her. In the end, therefore, Jim is using her as a source of pleasure for himself.

John Paul II says that if the interaction between a man and a woman remains at the level of these initial reactions produced by the sexual urge, the relationship is not able to grow into a true communion of persons. "Inevitably, then, the sexual urge in a human being is always in the natural course of things directed towards another human being—this is the normal form which it takes. If it is directed towards the sexual attributes as such this must be recognized as an impoverishment or even a perversion of the urge" (49).

This is an important point for our daily encounters with persons of the opposite sex. Following the personalist principle, John Paul II reminds us how careful we must be in order to avoid treating others as potential objects to enjoy for our own sensual or emotional pleasure. Along these lines, we must ask ourselves a crucial question: *What will we do when we experience the stirring of sexual attraction to a particular person of the opposite sex?* What will a man choose to do when he notices the physical beauty of a woman? What will a woman choose to do when she finds herself attracted to a man?

In these pivotal moments, we can choose to focus on the pleasure we receive from another person's body or from their masculinity or femininity. In so doing, we would be viewing the person as an object to enjoy and thus fall into utilitarianism. Or we can seek to cultivate authentic love for this man or woman, directing our attention to the *whole person*. By looking beyond the physical and psychological attributes and seeing the actual person, we open the door at least to the possibility of willing the good of the other, as in the virtuous friendship, and of performing truly selfless acts of kindness that are not dependent on the pleasure we receive from the relationship.

With these insights, John Paul II reminds us that our delicate interactions with persons of the opposite sex demand great responsibility. "For this very reason manifestations of the sexual urge in man must be evaluated on the plane of love, and any act which originates from it forms a link in the chain of responsibility, responsibility for love" (50). In the next few chapters, we will explore the pope's insights on how practically we can direct our attention to the person, not just their sexual attributes, in order to embrace authentic love and responsibility for those around us.

For Further Reading
Love and Responsibility, pp. 45–69

For Discussion and Reflection

1. John Paul II notes that some relationships are based more on mutual use—some pleasure or benefit each person receives from the other—than on a true commitment to each other and the pursuit of a common goal. Think about how couples who are dating or married tend to relate nowadays. What are some ways we see mutual use in relationships today?

2. Why do people in utilitarian relationships feel so much insecurity and instability? Have you ever observed this in others or even experienced this yourself? Do the pope's insights help you to better understand and come to terms with that experience?

3. What are some signals that a relationship is based more on mutual use than on committed love?

4. How is the sexual urge in human persons different from mere animal instinct? What does this difference tell us about the way we should respond when we experience physical or emotional attraction to a person of the opposite sex?

5. As John Paul II pointed out, "...if I treat someone else as a means and a tool in relation to myself I cannot help regarding myself in the same light" (39). How is this so? How do the dynamics in our relationships actually reflect our view of ourselves?

6. What does John Paul II mean when he says the sexual urge can provide the raw material for love? How is this so?

chapter three

Avoiding Fatal Attractions

A man eating lunch at a restaurant notices an attractive woman at another table and is immediately drawn to her beauty. His heart stirs, and he finds himself wanting to see her again.

This is not the first time she has caught his eye, and his attraction to her is more than physical. She works for the same large company, and he has been drawn to her warm personality, her cheerful smile, and her kindness toward others. He is taken in by her personality as much as by her natural beauty.

Basic attractions like this happen all the time between men and women. Sometimes we feel them very quickly. A man standing in line at a store may immediately be attracted to a woman walking by. A woman at church may notice a man praying after Mass and wonder about him the rest of the day. Sometimes, deeply felt attractions take longer to develop. A man and a woman who were friends or colleagues for several months may find themselves increasingly attracted to one another, emotionally and physically, over time.

In his book *Love and Responsibility,* John Paul II analyzes the anatomy of an attraction. What is really happening when men and women find themselves attracted to one another?

THE ANATOMY OF AN ATTRACTION

Let's begin by explaining a few of John Paul II's terms. At the most basic level, to attract someone means to be regarded by that person as a good (74). In turn, to *be* attracted to someone else means to perceive some value in that person, such as beauty, virtue, or personality, and to respond to that value. This attraction involves the senses, the mind, the will, the emotions, and desires.

> "...sensuality by itself is not love, and may very easily become its opposite" – St. John Paul II

The reason men and women are so easily attracted to each other is because of the sexual urge. Recall that the sexual urge is the tendency to seek the opposite sex. With the sexual urge, we are particularly oriented toward the physiological and psychological qualities of a person of the opposite sex—their body and their masculinity or femininity. John Paul II calls these physical and psychological qualities the *sexual values* of a person.

Therefore, a person is easily attracted to someone of the opposite sex in two ways: physically and emotionally. First, a man is attracted physically to the body of a woman, and a woman is attracted to the body of a man. The pope calls this attraction to the body *sensuality*.

Second, a man is also attracted emotionally to the femininity of a woman, and the woman is emotionally attracted to the masculinity of a man. John Paul II calls this emotional attraction *sentimentality*.

In the next chapter, we will consider the role of the emotions and sentimentality. Here, we will focus on the sensual attraction men and women experience for one another.

SENSE AND SENSUALITY

As we have seen, sensuality is concerned with the sexual value connected to the body of a person of the opposite sex. Such an attraction is not bad in itself because the sexual urge is meant to draw us not simply toward the body, but the body of a person. Hence, an initial sensual reaction is meant to orient us toward personal communion, not just bodily union. It can serve as an ingredient of authentic love if it is integrated with the higher, nobler aspects of love such as good will, friendship, virtue, or self-giving commitment (108).

Nevertheless, John Paul II says that sensual attractions, on their own, can lead to great dangers. First, "...sensuality by itself is not love, and may very easily become its opposite" (108).

"What's wrong with having lustful thoughts? I'm not hurting anyone when I do that!"

The reason sensuality can be so dangerous is that, on its own, it can easily fall into utilitarianism. When only sensuality is stirred, we experience the body of the other person as a potential object of enjoyment. We reduce the person to their physical qualities—their good looks, their body—and view the person primarily in terms of the pleasure we can experience from those qualities.

What is most tragic here is that sensual desire, which is meant to orient us toward communion with the person of the opposite sex, can actually keep us from loving that person. A man, for example, may sensuously ponder in his mind or actively seek the body of a woman as a means for sexual gratification. And he may do this without any real interest in her as a person. This focus on her sexual values keeps him from responding to her value as a person. This is why John Paul II says sensuality by itself is blind to the person. "Sensuality in itself has a 'consumer orientation'—it is directed primarily and immediately towards a 'body': it touches the person only indirectly, and tends to avoid direct contact" (105).

LOVE CHOCOLATE?

Second, John Paul II says sensuality on its own not only misses the person, it even fails to grasp the true beauty of the body. He explains how beauty is experienced through contemplation, not the stirring desire to exploit. When contemplating the splendor of a landscape, a sunset, a piece of music, or a work of art, we are taken in by the beauty. This contemplation of beauty brings peace and joy. This is very different from a consumer attitude to exploit an object for pleasure—an attitude that brings unrest, impatience, and an intense desire for satisfaction.

Perhaps an analogy will be helpful here. I once had the opportunity to see the work of a "chocolate artist." The artist had on display dozens of elaborate sculptures of ships, flowers, birds, towers, and buildings. What made these large sculptures so impressive is that they were all made of black, brown, and white chocolate.

There are two different attitudes I could have toward these chocolate sculptures. On one hand, I could gaze upon them as works of art, admiring their beauty and allowing myself to be taken in by their immensity, their perfect proportions, the intricate details, and the workmanship, marveling that these delicate masterpieces were made out of sugar and cocoa.

On the other hand, I could ignore the fact that these sculptures are beautiful pieces of art to be contemplated, and view them primarily as candies to be devoured—delicious chocolates that would satisfy my cravings. This latter approach, however, would be a degradation of the confectioner's masterpieces, reducing them to mere objects to be exploited for my tasting pleasure.

Similarly, sensuality on its own fails to see the human body as a beautiful masterpiece of God's creation, for it reduces the body to being an object to be exploited to satisfy one's own sensuous cravings. "Thus, sensuality really interferes with apprehension of the beautiful, even of bodily, sensual beauty, for it introduces a consumer attitude to the object: 'the body' is then regarded as a potential object of exploitation" (105–106).

MICHELANGELO AND *PLAYBOY*

This also helps explain one big difference between pornography and good classical art that depicts the nakedness of a person. Both *Playboy* magazine and art in the Vatican Museum, for example, may present the sexual organs of the human body. In fact, some in the pornography industry say their pictures are just another form of art, portraying the beauty of the body. Some defenders of pornography have even asked why the Church condemns pornography but allows nakedness depicted in its some of its own museums!

The pornography of *Playboy*, however, does not draw attention to the *beauty* of the human body. It draws attention to the body as an object to be used for one's own sexual satisfaction. In the end, it is a reduction of the human person to the sexual value of the body. On the contrary, good art depicting the body as beautiful is not a reduction of the person, but an enlarging of the person, leading us to contemplate the mystery of the human person as a masterpiece in God's creation.

Good art leads us to a peaceful contemplation of the true, the good, and the beautiful, including the truth, goodness, and beauty of the human body. Pornography, on the other hand, does not lead us to such contemplation, but instead stirs in us a sensuous craving for the body of another person as an object to be exploited for our own pleasure. Put simply, there probably aren't many people who have fallen into sin by gazing upon Michelangelo's famous portrayals of Adam and Eve in the Sistine chapel. But there probably aren't many who have *not* fallen into lustful thoughts when looking at pornographic pictures.[1]

> "The one who is looked at lustfully is not treated as a person, but as a body to be exploited for someone else's pleasure."

ENSLAVED TO SENSUALITY

A third reason John Paul II is concerned about sensuality is that if we leave this area of our lives unchecked, we will become enslaved to everything that stimulates our sensual desire. For example, a man given in to sensuality finds his will so weakened that he is led around by whatever sexual values appear most immediately to his senses. Whenever he encounters a woman dressed a certain way, he cannot help but glance at her with impure thoughts. Whenever he sees images of women on TV, on the Internet, or in magazines, he cannot resist looking at them, as he hankers after the sexual value of the woman and wants to enjoy the pleasure he can derive from his glances.

Especially in a highly sexualized culture like ours, we are constantly bombarded with sexual images exploiting our sensuality, getting us to focus on the bodies of members of the opposite sex. Indeed, we can easily find ourselves enslaved, bouncing from one sexual value to the next. As John Paul II points out, sensuality on its own "...is characteristically fickle, turning wherever it finds that value, whenever a 'possible object of enjoyment' appears" (108).

"I Can Look But Can't Touch"

Furthermore, in one of his most profound points in this section, the pope warns that we can use a person's body even when that person is not physically present. We do not need to see, hear, or touch another to exploit the other's body for our own sensuous pleasure. Through memory and imagination, we "...can make contact even with the 'body' of a person not physically present, experiencing the value of that body to the extent that it constitutes a 'possible object of enjoyment'" (108–109).

We live in a culture where many people say to themselves, "What's wrong with having lustful thoughts about someone else? I'm not hurting anyone when I do that!" Even some married people may think, "I'm not committing adultery when I look at another person this way. I'm still faithful to my spouse. I can look; I just can't touch." However, we must remember Christ's strong words about this matter: "Every one who looks at a woman lustfully has already committed adultery with her in his heart" (Matthew 5:28).

John Paul II's insights help explain what is really happening when men and women look lustfully at each other, and why consenting to impure thoughts and sexual fantasies is always morally wrong and so degrading to the other person. In the end, the one who is looked at lustfully is not treated as a person, but as a body to be exploited for someone else's pleasure.

Yet, as we have seen, sensuality alone is not love. It can be raw material for the development of true love, but this yearning for the sexual value of the body must be supplemented by other nobler elements of love, such as good will, friendship, virtue, total commitment, and self-giving love (themes we will consider in subsequent chapters). If sensuality is not carefully integrated with these higher elements of love, sensual desire will be harmful for a relationship. In fact, it can destroy love between a man and woman, and it can even prevent love from ever developing in the first place.

FOR FURTHER READING
Love and Responsibility, pp. 80–82, 101–109

FOR DISCUSSION AND REFLECTION

1. What are the two ways men and women are attracted to each other?
2. Is sensuality bad? What are some of the dangers of sensuality?
3. What are some practical ways we can avoid becoming enslaved to sensuality? How can men and women help each other guard against temptations in this area?
4. C.S. Lewis wrote:

> We use a most unfortunate idiom when we say of a lustful man prowling the streets, that he "wants a woman." Strictly speaking, a woman is just what he does not want. He wants a pleasure for which a woman happens to be the necessary piece of apparatus.... Now [love] makes a man really want, not a woman, but one particular woman. In some mysterious but quite indisputable fashion the lover desires the Beloved herself, not the pleasure she can give.[2]

How does this quote correspond with John Paul II's discussion of the "consumer attitude" of sensuality? In what ways does contemporary society promote a consumer mentality, as opposed to one that truly respects the dignity and value of the person?

5. What is wrong with pornography? How would you respond to someone who said pornography is just another form of art and there is nothing wrong in looking at it? Consider the following passage from the *Catechism of the Catholic Church*: "To the extent that it is inspired by truth and love of beings, art bears a certain likeness to God's activity in what He has created.... Art is not an absolute end in itself, but is ordered to and ennobled by the ultimate end of man [Cf. Pius XII, *Musicae sacrae disciplina*; Discourses of September 3 and December 25, 1950]" (CCC, 2501). In light of this, how does pornography fall short of the *Catechism*'s definition of art?

6. Commenting on the Gospel passage from Matthew 5:28, John Paul II warns against using someone's body even when that person is not physically present. What is morally wrong with someone having lustful thoughts about another person?

7. In his addresses known as the Theology of the Body, John Paul II makes a radical statement: "Man can commit...adultery in the heart also with regard to his own wife, if he treats her only as an object to satisfy instinct" (*TOB*, 157). Discuss how "adultery of the heart" might occur even within a married relationship.

8. How can married men and women strive to preserve inner integrity and purity in regard to their relationship with their spouses? Similarly, how can single people strive for this same purity of heart in relationships with members of the opposite sex, particularly in preparation for a vocation to either the married or religious life?

chapter four

Sense and Sentimentality:
The Proper Role of the Emotions

*H*ow could Mr. Right turn out to be so wrong?

Many young people have had the experience of *feeling* they were in love with someone who at first seemed absolutely wonderful, only later to become greatly disappointed in the person, disillusioned about the relationship, and perhaps even pessimistic about the opposite sex as a whole.

John Paul II explains why this often happens to men and women and how we can avoid such disillusionment in the future.

More Than Physical
In the last chapter, we considered one powerful aspect of the attraction between men and women: sensuality. We saw how this physical attraction is often characterized by a longing to enjoy the body of another person as an object of pleasure.

There is a second kind of attraction, however, that goes beyond physical desire for the body. John Paul II calls it *sentimentality*. This represents more of an emotional attraction between the sexes.

For example, when boy meets girl, in addition to noticing her "good looks," he also may find himself powerfully drawn to her femininity, her warm personality, her kindness—or as the pope calls it, her feminine "charm." Similarly, when girl meets boy, she not only may recognize that he is handsome, but also may find herself having strong feelings and admiration for his masculinity, his virtue, the way he carries himself—or as John Paul II calls it, his masculine "strength."

Such emotional reactions toward persons of the opposite sex happen all the time. We may experience sentimental affection for a spouse, a coworker, or a longtime friend. Or we may experience it toward a person we're introduced to at a meeting, a stranger we see at the mall, or even a fictional character we see on TV. Sentimentality can become part of what leads to authentic, selfless love for another person, but if we are not careful, we can easily become enslaved to our emotions in ways that prevent us from truly being able to love others.

A Sinking Ship

Love *should* integrate our emotions. In its fullest form, love is not a cold, calculated decision, devoid of feelings. A spouse saying, "Honey, I love you. I have no feelings at all for you, but know that I am committed to you," is not the ideal situation. Our emotions are meant to be caught up into our commitment to our beloved, thus enriching the relationship and giving us an even deeper experience of union with the other person (75).

As the pope explains, "Sentimental love keeps two people close together, binds them—even if they are physically far apart—to move in each other's orbit" (110). Consequently, "A person in this state of mind remains mentally always close to the person with whom he or she has ties of affection" (111).

John Paul II, however, is concerned that people today often think of love *only* in terms of feelings. His concerns seem all the more applicable in a culture like ours in which love songs, romance films, and TV shows constantly play with our emotions and prompt us to long for quick, emotionally thrilling relationships like the ones people seem to find in the movies.

Real love, however, is very different from Hollywood love. Real love requires much effort. It is a *virtue* that involves sacrifice, responsibility, and a total commitment to the other person. Hollywood love is an *emotion*. It's something that just happens to you. The focus is not on a commitment to another, but on what is happening inside you—the powerful, good feelings you experience when you're with this other person.

The *Titanic* phenomenon of the late 1990s demonstrates how many people have bought into the illusion of Hollywood love. Millions of young Americans returned again and again to experience the intensely emotional romance between the two main characters in this film—a romance that develops over just a few days between two people who really don't know each other and have no true commitment to each other. Yet viewers felt deeply that this attraction is the ideal kind of love that would have lasted a lifetime. With this kind of model to imitate, it's no wonder so many of our real life relationships are ending in shipwreck.

Of course, our feelings can and should be incorporated into a more fully developed love (a theme we will explore in subsequent chapters). However, when we are carried away by our emotions, we end up avoiding a very important question that is crucial for the long-term stability of a relationship: the question of truth. We must first and foremost consider the truth about the other person and the truth about the quality of our relationship: "What kind of character does this person really have?" "How strong is our relationship, really?" "Can this person shoulder a lot of responsibility in life?" "Is this the kind of person who will make sacrifices for me and put what's best for me or our family before himself?"

AVOIDING THE QUESTION OF TRUTH

One danger of making emotions a measure for love is that our feelings can be very misleading. In fact, the pope says feelings themselves are blind, for they are not concerned with knowing the truth about the other person. Thus, our feelings alone do not make a good compass for guiding our relationships.

He explains that we discover truth through using our reason. I know that two plus two equals four not because I *feel* it equals four. I come to certainty about this truth through my reason. Our feelings, on the other hand, do not have the job of seeking truth, the pope says.

Our feelings, therefore, will not be as helpful a guide for seeing the honest truth about another person and the truth about the quality of our relationship. "Feelings arise spontaneously—the attraction which one person feels towards another often begins suddenly and unexpectedly—but this reaction is in effect 'blind'" (77).

This becomes especially clear when we consider what happened to our emotions after the Fall. Before sin entered the world, man's intellect easily directed his will to choose what is good and to guide his emotions so that he would pursue the good with all his passions and emotions.

Since the Fall, however, the intellect does not see the truth clearly, the will is weakened in its resolve to pursue what is good, and our emotions are no longer properly ordered but go in many different directions. We now often experience much instability in the emotional sphere and many chaotic ups and downs—love and hate, hope and fear, joy and sadness—throughout our lives. Yet ironically, the modern view of love tells us to turn precisely to our feelings—to look right in the middle of this emotional roller coaster ride—to find an infallible measure of our love. No wonder there is so much confusion and instability in relationships today!

Is It Really So?

Furthermore, not only do feelings *not* have the task of seeking truth, but feelings also can be so powerful that they cloud the way we think about a person. John Paul II explains that when we are carried away by our emotions, sentimentality may hinder our ability to know that person as he or she really is.

This is why he stresses that in any emotional attraction, the question of truth about the person is crucial: "Is it really so?" We should be asking ourselves, "Does this person really have the qualities and virtues I'm so attracted to?" "Are we really as good a fit for one another as I feel we are?" "Is he or she truly worthy of all my trust?" "Is there a problem in our relationship that I'm overlooking?"

Our *feelings* do not address these important questions. In fact, our feelings often get us to avoid these questions, leaving us with a distorted and exaggerated perception of our beloved. (Note: In the following quote, John Paul II uses the philosophical term "subject" to refer to the human person.)

> This is why in any attraction—and, indeed, here above all— the question of the truth about the person towards whom it is felt is so important. We must reckon with the tendency, produced by the whole dynamic of emotional life, for the subject to divert the question "is it really so?" from the object of attraction to himself or herself, to his or her emotions. In these circumstances the subject does not enquire whether the other person really possesses the values visible to partial

eyes, but mainly whether the newborn feeling for that person
is a true emotion. (78)

This, again, does not mean that feelings are bad. But they cannot be
the primary criterion for discerning the honest truth about another
person or for clearly evaluating a relationship that we're in.

DATING LOSERS

Men and women often persist in relationships that, deep down,
they know are not good. They notice certain faults in the other
person. Problems begin to surface. Anxiety and insecurity take
over. They see the red flags but do nothing to end the relationship.

A lot of justification must take place. "When you're emotionally
attached," one young woman
explained, "you focus only on
the good. You overlook the
problems. You're quick to make
excuses for the other person."

> "If I wrote on a sheet of paper the
> things my girlfriends actually said,
> how they acted, and what they
> believed…there's no way I would
> have continued dating them."

This caused great difficulties
for another woman who was
dating someone in college. "I
started seeing how he treated his family and his roommate. Then
I started noticing how he was treating me. I sensed there were
problems, but I kept telling myself, 'He's not that bad. He's not
always like that.' But if I were on the outside and saw my friend
going through a relationship like that, I would have do all I could
to convince her to get out of it. But I gave my heart too much too
fast, and I couldn't see what was really going on."

One man says he regrets not using his head more than his
emotions to guide him in his dating relationships. He looks back
and wishes he had observed more how his girlfriends handled

conflict and stress, whether they lived to serve others or themselves, how they treated family and friends, and how they responded to things that were important to him. "If I had written on a sheet of paper the things my girlfriends actually said, what they did, how they acted, and what they believed, that would have been a big eye opener.... If I had simply read about them and asked, 'Is this the kind of woman I'd like to marry?' there's no way I would have continued dating them. But I never used my mind to look at their virtue. I just focused on their good looks or went with my emotions."

This tendency to be swept away by our emotions and to avoid questions of truth is characteristic of sentimental love. We are inclined to exaggerate the value of the person we have feelings for, downplaying their faults and ignoring any problems we have in the relationship.

John Paul II makes an amazing statement about how much our feelings can control our perception of the person to whom we're so attracted: "Thus, in the eyes of a person sentimentally committed to another person the value of the beloved object grows enormously—*as a rule out of all proportion to his or her real value*" (112, italics added).

Did you catch that? He doesn't say that in the beginning stages of sentimental love we might *sometimes* exaggerate the value of the person. He says this happens as a rule—we do it all the time! And he didn't say that we tend to exaggerate the person's value only slightly. We tend to idealize the value of the person "out of all proportion" to whom he or she is in reality.

This idealization can manifest itself in many ways. For example, a woman shows up at a Catholic young adult gathering and meets a devout man who exhibits three and a half of her favorite virtues and actually is somewhat good-looking. Though she just met him, she catches herself wondering, "Maybe this is the one!" and thinks about him throughout the week.

A young man who exaggerates his girlfriend's good qualities while ignoring many problems in their relationship may rush into marriage with the illusion of having found true love. When the real nature of their relationship becomes apparent, he says to himself, "I wish I had thought about this *before* I got married."

A married man not feeling close to his wife may develop an emotional attachment to another woman. He finds himself thinking about her often and going out of his way to see

> You've both only been taken in by the images you've carefully projected of yourselves—ideal images, not your true selves.

her. He idealizes this other woman, saying to himself, "*She* really understands me much better than my wife does."

Even a religious sister or priest might develop an emotional attraction to someone in a way that leads them to idealize the person. They begin to question their vocation and imagine a life with that person.

Social Media Romance

Social media makes it even easier for us to idealize others. We notice a person's photo, and it sparks a curiosity. We view their profile, look at other pictures, and read their posts. Soon we're "stalking" them. We barely know this person in real life, but from what we see on screens, we make him or her out to be a very special person we hope to date someday. We read a lot more into things than is really there. "Your brain can't help but fill in the gaps," one young adult explained. "You create a character in your head, but it's not the real person."

Many romantic relationships start out this way. Someone sends you a message. You respond. They craft a perfect response and seem very interesting, even though they may not be that way in person. It's easy to flirt and say things in a message that you'd never say face-to-face. Soon you share something personal, and they respond just the right way, with empathy or encouragement. You are becoming emotionally attached. Meanwhile, you find yourself giving a lot of thought as to what image you want to project of yourself: witty, compassionate, deep, fun. Next thing you know, you're in a romantic relationship even though you've not truly encountered the real person, and the other person has not gotten to know the real you. You've both only been taken in by the images you've carefully projected of yourselves—ideal images, not your true selves. In such a relationship, you will remain unsatisfied since you ultimately desire to be known and loved for who you really are.

EYES WIDE OPEN

Given our tendency to idealize, we must approach our relation-ships with the opposite sex with eyes wide open. Especially at the beginning stages of a relationship, if we naively say we're not idealizing the other person at all, it's probably a sign of how far we have already drifted from reality. In these early stages of love, if we are so quick to notice our favorite qualities in our beloved, we should be just as quick to admit that we are likely falling into the tendency to exaggerate these qualities. As John Paul II explains, "…a variety of values are bestowed upon the object of love which he or she does not necessarily possess in reality. These are ideal values, not real ones" (112).

Why do we tend to idealize those we're attracted to? These ideal values are the ones that we long, with all our heart, to find in another person someday. They exist in our deepest wishes, desires, and dreams. When we finally meet someone with whom there is the slightest bit of chemistry, our emotions tend to rapidly call up these ideal values and project them onto that person.

USING PEOPLE EMOTIONALLY

When we speak of a man using a woman, we tend to think in terms of him using her for sexual pleasure. John Paul II, however, highlights that men and women can use each other for *emotional* pleasure as well. A devoutly Christian man and woman can have a physically chaste dating relationship but can still be using each other for the good feelings they experience when together, for the emotional security of having a boyfriend or girlfriend, or for the pleasure they derive from imagining their wedding day, hoping the other person will finally be "the one."

If I fall into such sentimental idealization, my beloved is not truly the recipient of my affections. Rather, the other person represents an opportunity for me to enjoy these powerful emotional reactions stirring within my heart. In this case, I do not love the person but, rather, the ideal values I have projected onto her. I do not truly love the person for her own sake but use her for the emotional pleasure I derive from idealizing her. As John Paul II explains, the beloved who is idealized "...often becomes merely the occasion for an eruption in the subject's emotional consciousness of the values which he or she longs with all his heart to find in another person" (112). (Note again, John Paul here uses "subject" to refer to a human person.)

DISILLUSIONMENT

The most tragic effect of sentimental idealization is that we end up not really knowing the person we find so attractive. A man in sentimental love may seek to be close to his beloved, spend a lot of time talking with her, and even go to Mass with her and pray with her. If he has idealized her, though, in reality he remains quite distant from her: The powerful affection he feels depends not on her true value, but only on the ideal values he has projected onto her.

Inevitably, this unchecked sentimentality will end in great disillusionment. When the real person comes to the surface—with all her faults and weaknesses—she cannot live up to the ideal. The lover will become quite disappointed in the beloved (113). The strong feelings will wane, and there will not be much left for the relationship to stand on. Even though the couple may give every outward appearance of being emotionally close to each other, they remain in fact quite divided from each other (114).

"It was embarrassing to see how blind I was."

I've seen this with young people on college campuses who give the impression to each other and the rest of campus that they have a strong, intimate, and even very Catholic relationship. They may study together, eat meals together, walk arm-in-arm everywhere, and stay up late talking or praying the rosary together. When they break up two months later, everyone is shocked, including the couple. Yet no matter what external signs of closeness they manifested, if sentimentality and idealization were driving the relationship, they may not have really known each other personally even though they felt close.

John Paul II goes a step further. He points out that couples may even be using each other for the emotional pleasure they derive from such idealization. These kinds of relationships quickly fall into disillusionment, frustration, and maybe even hatred as the beloved can no longer provide the powerful rush of good feelings that came from the ideal that was projected onto them (113).

The disillusionment that follows idealization can also be painful. Relationships that seemed so promising at first suddenly end with great heartache. "I so badly wanted the relationship to work. I thought this was the one. That's why it was so terrifying for me to experience how hurt I could be by the one who I thought loved me," said one young adult after experiencing a very painful breakup. Others experience a lot of shame: "I was blind," said another young adult who idealized his girlfriend. "It was embarrassing to see how blind I was. My ego was shattered. I need to be more guarded next time."

In sum, sentimentality can be a beautiful, enriching part of love, but it must be integrated with other essential ingredients, or risk becoming the very opposite of love. In the next chapter, we will turn our attention to the single most important and most essential aspect of love in any relationship: self-giving.

For Further Reading
Love and Responsibility, pp. 73–80, 109–118

For Discussion and Reflection

1. C.S. Lewis wrote:

   Being in love is a good thing, but it is not the best thing. There are many things below it, but there are also things above it. You cannot make it the basis of a whole life. It is a noble feeling, but it is still a feeling.... Who could bear to live in that excitement for even five years?... But, of course, ceasing to be "in love" need not mean ceasing to love. Love in this second sense—love as distinct from "being in love"—is not merely a feeling. It is a deep unity, maintained by the will and deliberately strengthened by habit; reinforced by (in Christian marriages) the grace which both parents ask, and receive, from God. They can have this love for each other even at those moments when they do not like each other; as you love yourself even when you do not like yourself. They can retain this love even when each would easily, if they allowed themselves, be "in love" with someone else. "Being in love" first moved them to promise fidelity: this quieter love enables them to keep the promise. It is on this love that the engine of marriage is run; being in love was the explosion that started it.[1]

What is the difference between "being in love" and love itself? How is a deeper, quieter love, as Lewis calls it, actually better than "being in love"?

2. This chapter offered the example of the blockbuster movie *Titanic* as one that particularly played on the emotions of the audience. What are other examples of films, television shows, books, and music that overemphasize the sentimental aspect of love?

3. Why do you think this type of media tends to appeal so highly to our modern culture? What effect does the media's sentimental portrayal of love have on people and their relationships? How can you be more vigilant in your exposure to these distorted portraits of love in modern entertainment?

4. According to John Paul II, how much do we idealize people we find ourselves attracted to? What did John Paul II say about *why* we tend to idealize?

5. What effect does this idealization have on our relationships? Have you ever suffered disillusionment from being "blinded" by your emotions or feelings for another?

6. How can you guard against even unintentionally using others or being used by them emotionally?

7. According to John Paul II, women tend to struggle more with sentimentality. A woman's inherently sensitive nature, however, is part of what contributes to her true attractiveness and beauty. In his Apostolic Letter on the Dignity and Vocation of Women, John Paul II stated that, "Grace never casts nature aside or cancels it out, but rather perfects it and ennobles it."[2] How can women embrace those feminine qualities that make them unique, without becoming overly sentimental in their relationships? How can they help other women do the same?

8. What are the aspects of a potential romantic relationship that divert us from asking the crucial question, "Is it really so?" How can you strive to evaluate your relationships from a more integrated, truthful, and objective perspective?

chapter five

The Law of the Gift:
Understanding the Two Sides of Love

*T*he Italians have a beautiful expression for love: *ti voglio bene.* Though commonly translated as "I love you," *ti voglio bene* more literally means "I wish you good" or "I want what is good for you."

This phrase reminds us that love is not primarily about what good feelings may be stirring within. Even less is it about what I can get out of a relationship for myself. The fullness of love is looking outward toward my beloved and seeking what is best for that person, not just what is good for me. This, in fact, is how the *Catechism of the Catholic Church* defines love: "To love is to will the good of another" (CCC, 1766, quoting Thomas Aquinas, *Summa theologiae,* I–II, 24, 1). It's also a point John Paul II makes when he discusses the two sides of love: the subjective and objective.

According to John Paul II, understanding the difference between the subjective and objective is crucial for any married, engaged, or dating relationship. As we have seen in earlier chapters, the inner dynamic of emotional love (sentimentality) and physical desire (sensuality) largely shapes how men and women interact with each other, and it is what makes romance, especially in its early stages, so thrilling for the couple involved. John Paul II calls this first side of love the subjective aspect.

While this is one aspect of love, it is not to be equated with love in the fullest sense. We know from experience that we can have powerful feelings for another person without in any way being committed to them or without that person being committed to us in a relationship of selfless love.

This is why John Paul II puts the subjective aspect of love in its proper place. He wakes us up and reminds us that no matter how intensely we experience these sensations, it is not necessarily love, but simply "a psychological situation" (127). In other words, on its own, the subjective aspect of love is no more than a pleasurable experience happening inside of me. And these powerful sensations might actually conceal the reality of a relationship that has failed to develop fully.

> Will I really seek the good of my spouse, even when I don't feel like it? When I'm busy? When I'd rather be doing something else?

Turning Love Inward

Men and women today are quite susceptible to falling for this illusion of love, for the modern world has turned love inward, focusing primarily on the subjective aspect. John Paul II, however, emphasizes that there is another side of love that is absolutely essential no matter how powerful our emotions and desires may be. This is what he calls love's objective aspect.

This aspect has objective characteristics that go beyond the pleasurable feelings of the subjective level. True love involves virtue, friendship, and the pursuit of a common good. Both people are focused on a common goal outside of themselves. In Christian marriage, for example, a husband and wife unite themselves to the common aims of helping each other grow in holiness, deepening their own union, and raising children. Most of all, true love involves the selfless pursuit of what is best for the other person, even if it means sacrificing one's own preferences and desires— love in the sense of *ti voglio bene.*

When considering the objective aspect of love, I must discern what kind of relationship exists between my beloved and me *in reality*, not simply what this relationship means in my feelings. Am I committed to this other person for who she is or for the enjoyment I receive from the relationship? Does my beloved understand what is truly best for me, and does she have the faith and virtue to help me get there? Are we deeply united by a common aim, serving each other, and striving together toward a common good that is higher than each of us? Or are we just living side by side, sharing resources and occasional good times together while we selfishly pursue our own interests and enjoyments in life? These are the kinds of questions that get at the objective aspect of love.

Now we can see why John Paul II says that true love is "an interpersonal fact" (127), not just a "psychological situation" (127). A strong relationship is based on virtue and friendship: Unless a man and woman have the objective aspects of love in their relationship, they do not yet have a bond of true love.

Knowing the difference between these two aspects of love is crucial within marriage as well. What will spouses do in moments when the subjective feelings of love fade? A husband may not always have strong romantic feelings for his wife, but he is still called to serve her and make sacrifices for her. A woman may at times feel frustrated with her husband, but she must still honor and serve him. Will I really seek the good of my spouse, even when I don't feel like it? When I'm busy? When I'd rather be doing something else? Or what about when my spouse upsets me?

It's easy to love when we get a lot in return. But the objective aspect of love reminds us that true love is not merely about my experience of good feelings in marriage, but the commitment to seek what is best for the other person even when those feelings are not there—*ti voglio bene*. As John Paul II puts it, "...*love as experience should be subordinated to love as virtue*—so much so that without love as virtue, there can be no fullness in the experience of love" (120).

THE TWO SIDES OF LOVE

Subjective Aspect of Love	Objective Aspect of Love
"a psychological situation" (the feelings I experience)	"an interpersonal fact" (the relationship in reality)
Spontaneous reactions to sexual value based on: • Sensual attraction to the other's body • Emotional attraction to the other's masculinity/femininity	Union of persons based on: • Virtuous friendship • Pursuit of common good • Seeking what's best for the other • Self-giving love • Total commitment and sense of responsibility for the other person
Develops quickly	Develops over time
Arises spontaneously without much effort	Requires much effort and grace to cultivate virtuous, self-giving love

---

SELF-GIVING LOVE

One of the chief hallmarks of the objective aspect of love is the gift of self. John Paul II teaches that what makes betrothed (married) love different from all other forms of love such as attraction, desire, and friendship is that two people give themselves to each other. They are not just attracted to each other, and they do not simply desire what is good for each other. In betrothed love, each person surrenders himself entirely to the other. "When betrothed love enters into this interpersonal relationship something more than friendship results: two people give themselves each to the other" (96).

Yet the very idea of self-giving love raises some important questions: How can one person give himself to another? What does this mean? After all, John Paul II himself teaches that each human person is utterly unique. Each person has his own mind and his own free will. In the end, no one else can think for me. No one else can choose for me. Each person "is his own master" and is not able to be given over to another (125). So in what sense can one person give himself to his beloved?

John Paul II responds by saying that while on the natural and physical level it is impossible, *in the order of love* a person can do so by choosing to limit his freedom and uniting his will to the one he loves. In other words, because of his love, a person may actually *desire* to give up his own free will and bind it to the other person. Love "...makes the person want to do just that— surrender itself to another, to the one it loves" (125).

THE FREEDOM TO LOVE

For example, consider what happens when a man marries. As a single man, Bob is able to decide what he wants to do, when he wants to do it, and the way he wants to do it. He sets his own schedule. He decides where he lives. He can quit a job and move to another part of the country in an instant if he so desires. He can keep his apartment messy. He can spend his money as he pleases. He can eat when he wants, go out when he wants, and go to bed when he wants. He is used to making life decisions on his own.

Marriage, however, will significantly change Bob's life. If Bob decides on his own to quit his job, buy a new car, go on a weekend vacation, or sell the home, this is probably not going to go over very well with his wife! Now that Bob is married, all the decisions that he used to make by himself must be made in union with his wife and with a view to what is best for their marriage and family.

In self-giving love, men and women recognize in a profound way that their life is not their own. They have surrendered their will to their beloved. Their own plans, dreams, and preferences are not completely abandoned, but they are now put in a new perspective. They are subordinated to the good of the spouse and any children that may flow from their marriage. How they spend time and money and how they order their lives are no longer a matter of private choice. The marriage and the family become the primary reference points for everything they do.

This is the beauty of self-giving love: As single people, we have great autonomy and can in large part order our lives however we want. But men and women, driven by love, freely choose to give up their autonomy, to limit their freedom, by committing themselves to the good of the spouse. *Love is so powerful that it impels them to want to surrender their will to their beloved in this profound way.*

Indeed, many marriages today would be much stronger if only we understood and remembered the kind of self-giving love we originally signed up for: When we made our vows, we freely and lovingly chose to surrender our wills to our spouse. As John Paul II explains, "The fullest, the most uncompromising form of love consists precisely in self-giving, in making one's inalienable and non-transferable 'I' someone else's property" (97).

THE LAW OF THE GIFT

Now we come to the greatest mystery of self-giving love. At the heart of this gift of self is a fundamental conviction that in surrendering my autonomy to my beloved, I gain so much more in return. By uniting myself to another, my own life is not diminished but is profoundly enriched. This is what John Paul II calls the "law of ekstasis" or the law of self-giving: "...the lover 'goes outside' the self to find a fuller existence in another" (126).

> Love "makes the person want to do just that—surrender itself to another, to the one it loves."
> –St. John Paul II

In an age of vigorous individualism, however, this profound point from John Paul II may be difficult to understand. Our modern world emphasizes not self-giving love, but self-*getting* love, which focuses on what *I* get out of the relationship. Why should I go outside myself to find happiness? Why would I ever want to give up my autonomy and commit myself to someone else in this radical way? Why would I want to limit my freedom to do whatever I want with my life? These are the questions people ask today.

From a Christian perspective, however, life is not about doing whatever I want. It is about fulfilling my relationships with God and with the people God has placed in my life. In fact, this is where we find fulfillment in life: in living our relationships well. But to live our relationships well, we must often make sacrifices, surrendering our own will to serve the good of others.

This is why we discover a deeper happiness in life when we give ourselves in this way, for we are living the way God made us to live, which is the way God himself lives: in total, self-giving, committed love. As one of John Paul II's favorite lines from Vatican II says, "Man finds himself only by making himself a sincere gift to others."[1]

"Freedom exists for the sake of love." –St. John Paul II

SELF-GIVING OR SELF-GETTING LOVE?

This statement from Vatican II is especially applicable to marriage, where self-giving love between two human persons is seen most profoundly. In committing myself to another person in betrothed love, I certainly limit my freedom to do whatever I want. But at the same time, I open myself up to an even greater freedom: the freedom to love. As John Paul II explains:

> Love consists of a commitment which limits one's freedom—it is a giving of the self, and to give oneself means just that: to limit one's freedom on behalf of another. Limitation of one's freedom might seem to be something negative and unpleasant, but love makes it a positive, joyful and creative thing. *Freedom exists for the sake of love.* (135)

So we see that freedom is given for a purpose: for the sake of love. God gave us freedom so that we could choose to live for others, not just ourselves. The purpose of freedom is not to equip us to live a selfish life, slavishly pursuing whatever pleasurable desires come our way. We have freedom so that we can choose to make our lives a gift to God and others, committing ourselves to other persons, serving them and their needs.

Therefore, while the modern individualist may see self-giving love in marriage as something negative and restrictive, Christians view such limitations as liberating. What I really want to do in life is love my God, my spouse, my kids, and my neighbor—for in these relationships I find my happiness. And if I am to love my spouse and kids, I must be totally committed to them and free from having my selfish desires dictate my life and rule my household. If I am enslaved to always wanting to do whatever I feel like doing, it will not be easy for me to be generous with my spouse, be patient with my children, or make sacrifices for my family. It simply will not be easy for me to love them because I am habitually inclined to put my own preferences and desires above others.

That's why I must be free from the tyranny of doing whatever *I* want. Only then am I free to live the way God made me. Only then am I free to experience the happiness that comes in self-giving. Only then am I free to love.

FOR FURTHER READING

Love and Responsibility, pp. 82–100, 119–130

FOR DISCUSSION AND REFLECTION

1. In your own words, explain the distinction between the two sides of love—the subjective and the objective. How do these two aspects relate?

2. Read 1 Corinthians 13:4–7. How does this passage describe the objective side of love? Which attribute of the love St. Paul describes do you find most challenging or inspiring? What is one practical way you can strive to practice the virtue of love more in your everyday life?

3. What do you think John Paul II meant when he said, *"love as experience should be subordinated to love as virtue—so much*

so that without love as virtue there can be no fullness in the experience of love" (120)? What is the effect of making the subjective aspect of love the primary aspect of a relationship?

4. John Paul II said, "Love proceeds by way of this renunciation, guided by the profound conviction that it does not diminish or impoverish, but quite the contrary, enlarges and enriches the existence of the person" (125–126). How is it that when I surrender my freedom and give myself to another person, I actually gain so much more in return? How might we see the profound rewards of sacrificial, self-giving love played out in marriage and family life?

5. Matthew Kelly writes in his book *The Seven Levels of Intimacy*:

> But in order to love, you must be free, for to love is to give your *self* to someone or something freely, completely, unconditionally, and without reservation. It is as if you could take the essence of your very self in your hands and give it to another person. Yet to give your self—to another person, to an endeavor, or to God—you must first possess yourself. This possession of self is freedom. It is a prerequisite for love, and is attained only through discipline.
>
> This is why so very few relationships thrive in our time. The very nature of love requires self-possession. Without self-mastery, self-control, self-dominion, we are incapable of love....
>
> The problem is we don't want discipline. We want someone to tell us that we can be happy without discipline. But we can't.... The two are directly related.[2]

Why are discipline and self-renunciation a prerequisite for a genuine love? How can you specifically cultivate a habit of discipline in smaller areas of your life in order to gradually live the virtue of love in greater ways?

6. John Paul II wrote, "Freedom exists for the sake of love" (135). Have you ever experienced the mysterious freedom and joy that result from self-giving love—that is, choosing to go outside yourself for the sake of another? Describe your experience.

7. If you are married, how have you experienced the transition from living the single life to living a commitment to another person in self-giving love? Were these changes positive or negative? How have they helped you grow as an individual and as a couple? Or if you are currently discerning the vocation of marriage, what are some of the specific challenges and joys you anticipate as part of this particular call to self-giving love?

8. How is *every* person called to live self-giving love, whether one is single, married, or religious? What might this self-gift look like in the various states of life?

chapter six

Love and Responsibility?
Building Trust, Intimacy, and a Mature Love

*I*t is routinely pointed out that about half of all marriages end in divorce. But what is not often discussed is the other half of the equation: the marriages that don't break up. Are those marriages thriving? Do married couples that stay together feel truly close to one another? Do they achieve lasting, personal intimacy?

The picture on this other side of the divorce line is not a pretty one. Studies have shown that most couples do not feel as if they are married to a close friend. In fact, only about one out of ten married couples in America says they experience emotional intimacy in their relationship.[1]

A great marriage is not one that simply stays together, but one in which spouses experience deep personal communion with each other. We want marriages in which people ten, twenty, thirty years into married life can say, "I love my spouse more now than I did when we were first married."

For John Paul II, the key to personal communion in married life is mutual self-giving love and the accompanying sense of responsibility for each other as a gift. Indeed, this theme of responsibility is so important that he put it in the title of his book, calling it not simply *Love*, but *Love and Responsibility*.

What is this responsibility? And how can it transform relationships between spouses, engaged couples and significant others? That's what we will explore in this chapter's reflection.

RESPONSIBILITY

Think about what happens in married love. In our last reflection, we saw that the fullest sense of love involves two people giving themselves to each other. This self-giving is nothing less than a total entrusting of one's self to the other person—a surrendering of one's own preferences, freedom, and will for the sake of the other.

Since my beloved completely entrusts her life to me in this unique way, I must, in turn, have a profound sense of responsibility for her—for her well-being, her happiness, her emotional security, her holiness. As John Paul II explains, "There exists in love a particular responsibility—the responsibility for a person who is drawn into the closest possible partnership in the life and activity of another, and becomes in a sense the property of whoever benefits from this gift of self" (130).

Here, John Paul II offers a standard for love that is countercultural: "*The greater the feeling of responsibility for the person the more true love there is*" (131). Notice how he didn't say the more powerful the *emotions*, the more powerful the love is. Authentic love is not so self-centered and inward looking. Rather, true love looks outward in awe at my beloved who has entrusted herself to me, and it has a deep sense of responsibility for her good, especially in light of the fact that she has committed herself to me in this way.

ACCEPTING THE GIFT

In order to help us better appreciate the crucial role responsibility plays in a relationship, let's consider again the two aspects of self-giving love. On one hand, there is the giving of self: My beloved gives herself to me, and I give myself to her. On the other hand, there is the acceptance of the other person: I accept my beloved as a gift that has been entrusted to me, and she accepts me as a gift.

John Paul II notes how in betrothed love there is a great mystery of reciprocity in the giving and the receiving of each other. In fact, he makes a very intriguing statement about this: "...acceptance must also be giving, and giving receiving" (129).

How can acceptance be giving? In what sense is the acceptance of my beloved an actual gift to her? John Paul II's insights from his Theology of the Body will be helpful here.[2] While commenting on the marriage of Adam and Eve, he explains that when Eve was first given to Adam, he fully accepted her and the two became intimately united as one. "Then the man said, 'This at last is bone of my bones and flesh of my flesh'.... Therefore a man leaves his father and his mother and clings to his wife, and they become one flesh" (Genesis 2:23–24, NRSV-CE).

> "The greater the feeling of responsibility for the person the more true love there is."

Because sin had not yet entered the world, Adam did not struggle with selfishness. He loved his wife not for what he could get out of the relationship—a coworker in the garden, companionship, emotional pleasure, sexual pleasure. Rather, he loved her for who she was *as a person*. He accepted his wife as a tremendous gift that he would treasure and care for. He had a profound sense of *responsibility* for her, and he always sought what was best for her, not just his own interests. He never did anything that would hurt her. It's as if Adam carefully held her heart in the palms of his hands, sensing the full weight of the gift entrusted to his care.

THE KEY TO INTIMACY IN MARRIAGE

Put yourself in Eve's shoes. Imagine having a spouse like that! Imagine how she must have felt, being totally accepted in this way. Indeed, having a husband joyfully receive her as a gift and love her for her own sake was a great gift *to her*, for now her longing for personal communion could be fulfilled.

Adam's total acceptance of Eve provides her with the security she needs to feel safe enough to entrust her heart, indeed her whole life, fully to him without any fear of being let down. In other words, his committed love and acceptance of her fosters in her the trust that makes emotional intimacy possible.

This is the key to personal communion in marriage. Since Eve had complete trust in Adam's love for her, she never felt afraid of being used by him, being misunderstood by him, or being hurt by him. Therefore, in this context of committed love and responsibility, she felt free to give herself fully to her husband— emotionally, spiritually, physically—holding nothing back.

The same, of course, is true in the other direction. Eve's total acceptance of Adam as a gift similarly serves as a gift for him, further strengthening trust and intimacy in their relationship.

BACK TO THE GARDEN

This is the kind of dynamic we want for our marriage: one of total trust, which makes personal intimacy possible. But my beloved will grow to trust me—and thus unveil her heart to me— only to the extent that she senses that I am committed to her, that I totally accept her, and that I feel great responsibility for what is best for her.

This is not an easy thing to achieve. Unlike Adam and Eve in the garden, we are fallen. We are selfish and often do things to hurt one another, which can break down trust and thus hinder intimacy. For example, when a man is more preoccupied by what he needs to do at work than he is about caring for his wife's needs, he sends a message to her that she is not a priority, that everything else is more important. This, of course, doesn't help build trust and only makes her feel more distant from her husband.

> "Some people tell themselves, if I had married someone else, I know I wouldn't be treated this way."

Similarly, a wife who constantly nags her husband and criticizes him for his weaknesses, for not getting things done around the house, or for not having a better job may make him feel disrespected or unappreciated. Such complaining will likely only drive him further away from her emotionally.

Our Beloved's Faults

What about when we experience firsthand our beloved's weaknesses and feel hurt by something he or she has done? When we're hurt, we're tempted to get frustrated with our beloved, saying to ourselves, "Why does he always do this? He's never going to change!" We may become defensive: "This was not my fault! Why doesn't she *understand*?" We might put up walls: "I'm not going to tell him what I'm really feeling anymore. He doesn't care anyway." We might even begin to withdraw our love: "If I had married someone else, I know I wouldn't be treated this way."

John Paul II reminds us that at moments like these, our acceptance and responsibility for the other person is tested the most. Still, we should "love the person complete with all his or her virtues and faults, and up to a point independently of those virtues and in spite of those faults" (135). He's not saying we should condone or ignore the sins and weaknesses of our beloved, but he is challenging us to avoid viewing our beloved through the lenses of a prosecuting attorney. Even though we are hurt, we need to look beyond the mere legal facts—"She did this to me!"—and see the person, who maintains great value even in the midst of shortcomings and sins. After all, as we have seen throughout these reflections, true love is directed to the person—not just what he does for me. So when the beloved is having a not-so-beautiful moment, is not pleasing to me, and in fact does something to hurt me, will I still offer total love and acceptance?

TOTAL ACCEPTANCE OF YOUR SPOUSE

This is the kind of question that gets at the real measure of one's love. As John Paul II sums up,

> The strength of such a love emerges most clearly when the beloved person stumbles, when his or her weaknesses or even sins come into the open. One who truly loves does not then withdraw his love, but loves all the more, loves in full consciousness of the other's shortcomings and faults, and without in the least approving of them. For the person as such never loses its essential value. The emotion which attaches itself to the value of the person remains loyal to the human being. (135)

I remember a time when my wife exhibited this kind of committed love right after I had said something that hurt her. We were in the kitchen talking while she was putting several cans of food away, one by one, in a cabinet above. As soon as the words came out of my mouth, I regretted them. But there the words went, floating out in space toward my wife, sharpened by a certain tone in my voice—and there was absolutely nothing I could do to get them back. Judging from the look on her face, I knew they had reached her ears, and I knew that she was hurt.

She immediately stopped what she was doing, put the soup can in her hand back on the counter, looked down, and paused to take a breath. What was going to happen next?

To my surprise, though she was clearly hurt, she turned to me with a gentle smile and said, "You didn't *really* mean that, did you?"

When we're hurt by our beloved, we tend to turn inward and focus on our own feelings and respond with anger or resentment. However, my wife in this instance looked beyond the legal violation—I said something hurtful—and realized that I probably didn't really mean what I had said and that I already was feeling very badly about saying it.

Indeed, her rising above her hurt feelings gave me the opportunity to apologize, which I quickly did, and then she could forgive me. She did not ignore the fact that I hurt her or condone my words in any way. Yet rather than respond in a manner that would have escalated the tension, her acceptance of me even in the midst of the hurt I inflicted enabled us to be quickly reconciled, and we were able to move on with our lives and enjoy the rest of our evening together.

The Way God Loves Us

The kind of total acceptance that John Paul II says spouses should have for each other is, of course, analogous to the way the Lord loves us. Despite our many sins and failures, God remains committed to us, looking at us patiently and mercifully in the face of our faults. He loves us even when we do things that hurt our relationship with him.

This radical divine love for us is seen most powerfully in the Eucharist, as Jesus gives himself to us, his very Body and Blood, in Holy Communion. But John Paul II encourages us to think about the mystery of Holy Communion from the other angle as well: "We can say not only that *each of us receives Christ*, but also that *Christ receives each of us.*"[3] Think about that: When we receive Holy Communion in the state of grace, God not only gives himself to us in the Eucharist, but he also *receives us* into his divine life. And he receives us as we are—with all our shortcomings, weaknesses, and sins.

Therefore, if we wish to be more Christlike in our marriages, we must first and foremost develop a deeper attitude of love and acceptance for our spouse *as he or she is*, with all the imperfections. Instead of trying to change our beloved or becoming irritated with these faults, we must remain firmly committed to our husband or wife as persons who have been entrusted to us as a gift. Our fundamental attitude toward the beloved in the midst of weaknesses must not be one of agitation, defensiveness, or annoyance, but one of unwavering acceptance in our hearts for the other, bearing patiently with all the faults. When we do this, we begin to love as God loves.

Putting Love to the Test

Now we can see even more clearly that true love is not something that we just happen to stumble into. Despite our culture's depiction of love as something two people simply discover, complete and packaged from the start, John Paul II reminds us that authentic love requires much effort, virtue, and sacrifice. If we are to love the way God loves us, our initial experience of love must mature. No matter how powerfully we may experience certain feelings, desires, and emotions, these must be molded and integrated with the other higher, objective aspects of love.

In fact, John Paul II says that love is put to the test specifically when those powerful feelings grow weaker—when the sensual and emotional responses start to lose their effect. "Nothing then remains except the value of the person, and the inner truth about the love of those concerned comes to light" (134).

At this point, the reality of the relationship can no longer be disguised. Its true nature will come out into the open. If a couple's love is based on a true gift of self and a commitment to each other as persons, the relationship, "will not only survive but grow stronger, and sink deeper roots" (134). However, if the relationship was nothing more than two people coming together for sensual or emotional experiences, the relationship will no longer have any foundation on which to stand once those feelings fade into the background. In this kind of relationship, "the persons involved in it will suddenly find themselves in a vacuum" (134).

> She turned to me and said, "You didn't *really* mean that, did you?"

This is why it is important for love to be built on self-giving and responsibility—the objective aspect of love that we discussed in the previous chapter. This is the only way for love to mature and to endure.

IMMATURE LOVE

Finally, in this section, John Paul II steps back and looks at the big picture of what he has covered so far in *Love and Responsibility.* And he does this by highlighting the difference between a mature love and a love that has failed to mature.

When love is immature, the person is constantly looking inward, absorbed in his own feelings. Here, the subjective aspect of love reigns supreme. He measures his love by the sensual and emotional reactions he experiences in the relationship. Since these feelings themselves are unstable and constantly changing, however, a relationship that is based merely on these subjective aspects will follow the ups and downs of these feelings.

A mature love, however, is one that looks outward. First, it looks outward in the sense that it is based not on my feelings but on the honest truth of the other person and on my commitment to the other person in self-giving love. The emotions still play an important part, but they are grounded in the truth of the other person as he or she *really* is (not my idealization of that person). "The emotion becomes serene and confident, for it ceases to be absorbed entirely in itself and attaches itself instead to its object, to the beloved person" (134).

Here we see the proper role of the emotions in a relationship. When my subjective feelings are grounded in the objective truth about the other person, my emotions themselves take on a new quality and become integrated with authentic love. The emotions become "simpler and soberer" (134), John Paul II says. Having moved beyond the idealization of emotional love, the mature love based on a commitment to the other person "is concentrated on the value of the person as such and *makes us feel emotional love for the person as he or she really is, not for the person of our imagination, but for the real person*" (135, emphasis added).

Second, a mature love looks outward in the sense that the person actively seeks what is best for the beloved. The person with a mature love is not focused primarily on what feelings and desires may be stirring inside him. Rather, he is focused on his responsibility to care for his beloved's good. He actively seeks what is good for her, not just his own pleasure, enjoyment, and selfish pursuits.

A Tale of Two Marriages

A true story about two married couples I once knew—I've changed their names to protect their privacy—illustrates the sharp difference between an immature love and a love that has reached maturity. Both couples were living in the same town, at the same time, and faced similar trials in their relationships.

Phil and Lorraine had two children and had been happily married for several years when Lorraine was diagnosed with cancer. Her condition worsened quickly and soon she could move around only in a wheelchair. This was not at all what Phil was dreaming of when he married Lorraine. Not only did he face much unexpected financial and emotional stress, but also, he now needed to serve his wife and children in a sacrificial way that would take a lot out of him, not giving much pleasure in return.

Unwilling to rise to the challenge of self-giving love, Phil abandoned his wife and kids to pursue what he believed would be an easier life. He chose not to live out the commitment he made to Lorraine on their wedding day. Before the cancer hit, Phil gave the appearance of loving his wife. When tested by this crisis, however, the true nature of his love became apparent: It was not a mature love based on self-giving. It was a love centered on himself.

A few blocks away lived another married couple, Doug and Michelle, who faced a similar trial. Michelle came down with a form of multiple sclerosis that quickly led to her confinement in a wheelchair. Her condition was more disabling than Lorraine's. Michelle could no longer move her arms or hold up her head. She even lost the ability to talk.

Through her years of suffering, Doug remained by her side, serving her. In fact, in order to attend to his wife full-time, he decided to retire seven years early from a career he loved. And he did this knowing that he would not have as much money for himself during his own golden years.

As he watched his wife's condition worsen, Doug spent his days bathing her, feeding her, reading to her, and taking her outside for walks in the wheelchair. He continued to talk to her every day, even though she couldn't say anything back. For years, he couldn't have even one conversation with his wife.

Though there probably were not a lot of emotional highs in those days, Doug lovingly lived out his commitment to his wife to the end. When tested by this ordeal, Doug's love didn't fade but shone more brightly than ever before. It was a true, mature love—based not on his own enjoyment, but on the gift of himself and on his commitment to what would be best for his wife, no matter what the cost.

This is what marriage is all about. This is the kind of mature love John Paul II calls us to pursue, one in which responsibility for the other person is the chief hallmark. Do I have this profound sense of responsibility for my own spouse right now, day-to-day? Do I make it a priority to seek what is truly best for my spouse? Or am I too preoccupied by my own concerns, my own happiness, my own pursuits?

When we encounter a love of total self-giving, a love like Doug's, we come in contact with the love of Christ himself, radiating through his people on earth. It challenges us to take a closer look at the way we live our own marriages and inspires us to love and serve our spouses even more.

Is Your Love Mature?

Immature Love	Mature Love
Subjective Aspect is Primary	Objective Aspect is Primary
• Based on my feelings (sensual and emotional experiences)	• Based on the truth of the other person and my commitment to that person in self-giving love
Looking Inward	Looking Outward
• At my own feelings	• At the other person and his or her good
Causes Anxiety	Creates Confidence and Serenity
• Because based on my unstable feelings	• Because based on simpler, sober emotions—feel emotional love for the person as he really is
Egoism (Selfishness)	Altruism (Self-Giving)
• Focused on my own sensual and emotional enjoyment	• Focused on integrating sensual/emotional experiences with the objective aspects of love—virtuous friendship, self-giving, responsibility for the other person, a commitment to will what is best for the other person

FOR FURTHER READING
Love and Responsibility, pp. 130–140

FOR DISCUSSION AND REFLECTION

1. John Paul II says the greatest measure for love is a sense of responsibility for the other person. "The greater the feeling of responsibility for the person, the more true love there is" (131). What does it mean to feel responsibility for the other person? Why is this the true measure for love?

2. Catholic philosopher Alice von Hildebrand wrote:

> Conjugal love, like romantic love, wants to be heroic; but it does not limit arbitrarily the scope of this heroism. In its desire to relate itself existentially to heroism, it will find it also in the modest deeds of everyday life, and will transform the tiresome routine of daily duties into golden threads binding oneself closer and closer to the beloved. There is in conjugal love a note of truth which is lacking in romantic love. It is a love that has been tested in the furnace of everyday trials and difficulties and has come out victoriously.... To be kind and loveable for a moment is no great feat. But to be loving day after day in the most varied and trying circumstances can be achieved only by a man who truly loves.[4]

How can a deeper sense of responsibility for the beloved enable one to faithfully perform the daily, humble, heroic acts of authentic love that marriage requires?

3. John Paul II writes about how self-giving love and the receiving of the other person interpenetrate. How is acceptance of the other person as a gift in itself a gift to the other person?

4. For women: Reflect on the following quote from John Paul II: "A woman is capable of truly making a gift of herself only if she fully believes in the value of her person and in the value as a person of the man to whom she gives herself" (129). How do some women struggle in recognizing that they are intrinsically valuable, a valuable gift? How can you deepen your belief in the value of your own person?

   For men: Reflect on the following quote from John Paul II: "And a man is capable of fully accepting a woman's gift of herself only if he is fully conscious of the magnitude of the gift—which he cannot be unless he affirms the value of her person. Realization of the value of the gift awakens the need to show gratitude and to reciprocate in ways which would match its value" (129). How can you show deeper gratitude and awe at the magnitude of the gift of other persons and avoid taking others for granted within your relationships?

5. As chapter six pointed out, *trust* grows within the context of a truly committed relationship, one where each person is responsibly cared for and totally accepted. What are some practical ways to cultivate a greater atmosphere of trust within your relationships or your marriage? What are some things we do or say that break down trust in a relationship? How can we work to heal areas in which the seeds of distrust may have already been sown?

6. John Paul II wrote poignantly about how genuine love is measured when the beloved's weaknesses or even sins come to light. What is your typical reaction to others' shortcomings? How can you maintain a truly loving attitude without approving of others' faults?

7. Consider the following quote from Christian philosopher Søren Kierkegaard:

> Christ's love for Peter was so boundless that in loving Peter he accomplished loving the person one sees. He did not say, "Peter must change first and become another man before I can love him again." No, just the opposite, he said, "Peter is Peter, and I love him; love, if anything will help him to become another man." ...Christian love grants the beloved all his imperfections and weaknesses and in all his changes remains with him, loving the person it sees.[5]

How have you experienced healing and growth through someone's consistent love of you, despite your own failings? Are you impatient with your beloved's weaknesses—do you tend to want your beloved to change before you love him or her? How might showing the kind of love Christ showed Peter actually be more helpful? What are some practical ways you can do that?

chapter seven

Resenting Chastity: The Current Crisis

Virtue is not simply something lacking in the modern world. It is something many in the modern world actually *resent*. John Paul II makes this point when beginning his teaching on chastity in *Love and Responsibility.*

Why do so many today resent virtue? Living the virtuous life is not easy. It requires constant effort, practice, and self-denial as we battle against our fallen, selfish human nature. On this side of the Garden of Eden, it's much easier to give in to our emotions and desires than it is to control them. It is easier to indulge our appetite, for example, than to eat with moderation. It is easier to lose our temper when things don't go our way than it is to moderate our anger. It is easier to give in to discouragement and complaining than to joyfully endure our trials with patience.

The virtues remind us of the higher moral standard we are called to follow. This reminder should inspire us to give more of ourselves in the pursuit of virtue and live more like Christ, rather than living life enslaved by our passions.

But not everyone wants to be reminded of this! For souls not wanting to give up certain pleasures or comforts—souls not wanting to do the work and make the sacrifices necessary to grow in virtue—any discussion of the virtues can be like a mirror reflecting back to them their own moral laziness.

Virtue Subverted

That's why some people resent the virtues. Instead of being inspired to live a better life, they tear down the moral standard of the virtues and drag it down to their own level. In other words, they minimize the significance of the virtues in order to spare themselves the effort and to excuse their own moral failures.

Imagine, for example, several women working in an office who gossip and talk about other people behind their backs. One of their Christian colleagues, however, does not participate in their gossip. Instead of being inspired by her example, her coworkers make fun of her. They ridicule her as being a holy roller who is "too good for the rest us." Rather than praise her virtue, they tear it down and *resent* it.

Similarly, imagine the college student who studies diligently, always does his assignments, and doesn't go to parties with the other men on his dorm floor. Instead of praising his virtue, his peers ostracize him and view him as a boring nerd who never has any fun. By not going along with what everyone else is doing, he stands as a reminder of their own laziness and immoral behavior. And so they *resent* his virtue.

One last example: The world today deeply resents the virtue of faith. Pope Benedict XVI once pointed out that many people today marginalize and brand as fundamentalist those who have a strong faith based on the creed or who have convictions about what is morally right or wrong. Rather than be inspired by people who have good religious and moral convictions, the modern world tends to ridicule such people, labeling them as conservative, rigid, judgmental, and intolerant. The virtue of faith is now seen as something evil in the world. It is not admired. It is *resented.*

John Paul II says many people devalue the virtues in order to excuse themselves from having to live by a higher standard. Since they don't want to make the effort to change, they treat the virtues lightheartedly or even openly attack them in order to justify their own lack of moral character. He explains that resentment "not only distorts the features of the good but devalues that which rightly deserves respect, so that man need not struggle to raise himself to the level of the true good, but can 'lightheartedly' recognize as good only what suits him, what is convenient and comfortable for him" (144).

RESENTING CHASTITY

The virtue that is probably resented most today is chastity. According to John Paul II, chastity is the virtue that frees love from utilitarian attitudes. "The essence of chastity consists in quickness to affirm the value of the person in every situation, and in raising to the personal level all reactions to the value of 'the body and sex'" (171). Thus, chastity helps purify our hearts of selfish desires and makes selfless, mature love between two persons possible. Today, however, chastity is no longer seen as something good, something noble, something we should all pursue. Just the opposite: Chastity is often portrayed as something evil—something *harmful* for human persons.

> Any discussion of the virtues can be like a mirror reflecting back to them their own moral laziness.

Some argue that chastity is damaging to the psychological health of young men and women. Sexual desire is natural, they say. Therefore, it is unnatural to restrict it in any way. After all, "a young man must have sexual relief" (144).

Others say chastity is an enemy of love. If two people love each other, shouldn't they be able to express their love through sexual intercourse? Chastity might have a role to play in other areas of life, but when two mutually consenting adults are in love, the restrictions of chastity are a tremendous hindrance to the couple expressing their love sexually.

These and many other arguments against chastity reflect our culture's resentment of this virtue. We witness this resentment in many college classrooms, in many sex education programs, and especially in the media. When a Hollywood film or prime-time comedy portrays romantic relationships, how often is chastity held up as a moral ideal? How often is chastity presented as something that makes us happy, as something the heroes intentionally make a priority in their lives?

In the rare show that might actually have a character who is deliberately striving to live a chaste life, how is she portrayed? As beautiful, fun, and intelligent? In practically every case, the rare chaste character is portrayed as an awkward, judgmental, naive, or repressed woman whom no one would ever want to imitate— unless, of course, the director makes her in the end come of age and discover her "true self" precisely by shedding her traditional moral values and losing her virginity.

WHY THIS RESENTMENT?

John Paul II says the main reason modern man views chastity as an obstacle to love is that we associate love primarily with the emotions or the sexual pleasure we receive from the person of the other sex. In other words, we tend to think of love only in its *subjective* aspect. As John Paul II has shown, however, a true, lasting love needs a much stronger foundation. It must be based on virtue, a commitment to the other person's good, and mutual self-giving—in other words, the *objective* aspect of love.

Therefore, the real questions in love are not the subjective ones: "Do I have strong feelings and desire for my beloved?" "Does he or she have strong feelings and sensual desire for me?" Anyone can have feelings and desire for another person. But not everyone has the virtue and commitment to make self-giving love possible.

Yet since the subjective aspect of love develops more rapidly and is felt more intensely than the objective aspect, many people confuse the feelings of love with love itself. On the objective level, it takes a lot of time and effort to cultivate a virtuous friendship. Relationships centered on total self-giving love and on a profound sense of responsibility for the other as a gift don't just happen spontaneously.

On the other hand, with the subjective aspect of love, it doesn't take much time and effort at all to experience sensual desire or emotional longing for a person of the opposite sex. Such reactions can happen in an instant. Furthermore, these sensual and emotional responses can be so powerful that they dominate how we view the other person.

In our fallen human nature, we can tend to see persons of the opposite sex primarily through the prism of their sexual values—the values that give us pleasure. As a result, we obscure our perception of them as persons and view them more as opportunities for our own enjoyment (159).

Our Tendency to Use the Opposite Sex

John Paul II points out that our encounters with the opposite sex are often mixed with this kind of emotional or sensual egoism—with a desire to use the person for our own emotional pleasure or sexual satisfaction. "The truth of original sin explains a very basic and very widespread evil—that *a human being encountering a person of the other sex does not simply and spontaneously experience 'love,' but a feeling muddied by the longing to enjoy"* (161, emphasis added).

Did you catch that? John Paul II is saying that when we encounter someone of the opposite sex—a stranger, a friend, a coworker, a boyfriend, a girlfriend, a spouse, or even another person's spouse—we should not expect a purely selfless attitude of Christian kindness to spontaneously spring from our hearts. Because we are fallen, our many complex attractions are often tainted by a selfish attitude of wanting to be with the other person *not* for the sake of any commitment to his or her well-being, but for the rush of good feelings or sensual pleasure we may receive from being with that person.

> Chastity is what makes love possible.

In other words, when boy meets girl, they do not automatically fall into authentic, self-giving, committed love for each other. That is why we need a virtue that helps us integrate our initial sensual and sentimental attractions with authentic love for the other as a person. Chastity is the virtue that enables us to love in this way. As John Paul II says: "Since sensations and actions springing from sexual reactions and the emotions connected with them tend to deprive love of its crystal clarity—a special virtue is necessary to protect its true character and objective profile. This special virtue is chastity, which is intimately allied to love between man and woman" (146).

CHASTITY: THE GUARDIAN OF LOVE

Now we can see why chastity is so necessary for love. Far from something that hinders our love, chastity is what makes love possible. It protects love from falling into selfish, utilitarian attitudes and enables us to love selflessly—irrespective of the powerful emotions or sensual delight we may receive from our beloved.

If we are to truly love a person of the opposite sex, we must see their full value as a person and respond to them in selfless love. John Paul II says chastity allows us to do just that. "The essence of chastity consists in quickness to affirm the value of the person in every situation, and in raising to the personal level all reactions to the value of 'the body and sex'" (171).

> "Only the chaste man and the chaste woman are capable of true love." —St. John Paul II

Men and women without chastity are in a very sad situation: They are not free to love. They may have good intentions and a sincere desire to care for the beloved, but without chastity, love will never flourish for it will not be pure. It will be mixed with a tendency to view the beloved primarily in terms of sexual values. John Paul II explains that without chastity, men and women cannot selflessly love the beloved as a *person* because the heart is so preoccupied with emotional and sensual pleasure (164).

But chastity protects love from falling into such utilitarianism; freed from utilitarian attitudes, the chaste are thus free to love. Thus also "only the chaste man and the chaste woman are capable of true love. For chastity frees their association, including their marital intercourse, from that tendency to use a person which is objectively incompatible with 'loving kindness,' and by so freeing it introduces into their life together and their sexual relationship a special disposition to 'loving kindness'" (171).

Now that we see the great importance of chastity for protecting love, we can turn our attention in the next chapter to John Paul II's practical strategies for putting chastity into practice.

FOR FURTHER READING
Love and Responsibility, pp. 143–158

FOR DISCUSSION AND REFLECTION

1. What are some ways we see the virtues mocked today? According to John Paul II, why are virtues often resented? Have you ever experienced resentment or even persecution for your pursuit of virtue? What was your response?

2. In what ways have you seen the virtue of chastity mocked or disregarded in contemporary culture? How do these false images and ideas distort the truth about chaste love?

3. John Paul II says that when men and women find themselves attracted to each other, their attraction is tainted by a desire to use each other sensually or emotionally. Because of original sin, "a human being encountering the opposite sex does not simply and spontaneously experience love, but a feeling muddied by a longing to enjoy" (161). Do you think this is true? Explain.

4. Ultimately, genuine love is greater than fleeting romance. How can living a life of chastity be its own reward? How does chastity protect love and make love possible?

5. Reflect on this verse from St. Paul: "Be blameless and innocent, children of God without blemish in the midst of a crooked and perverse generation, among whom you shine as lights in the world, holding fast the word of life" (Philippians 2:15–16).

   How do you think a positive, integrated vision of chastity could be more effectively promoted in the midst of our own "crooked and perverse generation"? What can be done within your own life, family life, the Church, schools, and work environments?

chapter eight

The Battle for Purity

*T*he battle for purity ultimately is fought deep in the recesses of the human heart. Our hearts were made to love, but since the Fall, they have been tainted by a desire to use others. In this reflection, we will see that chastity is so much bigger than simply saying no to certain sexual actions we may commit in the body. In the end, chastity is a matter of the heart.

CHASTITY: ONE LONG NO?

Chaste literally means *clean*: Christians have long used this word to describe the particular virtue that moderates our sexual desire. But this is *not* because sexual desire itself is somehow unclean or dirty. In fact, John Paul II warned against a negative view of chastity that turns this virtue into a mere suppression of sensual desire—"Just don't have sex before you're married!" In this negative light, chastity becomes merely "one long 'no'" (170). This kind of suppression can have serious consequences for the human person:

> Chastity is very often understood as a "blind" inhibition of sensuality and of physical impulses such that the values of the "body" and of sex are pushed down into the subconscious, where they await an opportunity to explode. This is an obviously erroneous conception of the virtue of chastity,

which, if it is practiced only in this way, does indeed create the danger of such "explosions." (170)

We must see chastity as a positive virtue that enables us to love and protects love from being tainted by the selfish tendency to use the other person for our own pleasure. John Paul II said chastity is emphatically *not* "one long 'no.'" Rather, it is first and foremost a yes—a yes in our heart to the other person, not just to his or her sexual values. It is a yes that requires us to say no to other things in order to protect love from falling into utilitarianism.

PURE LOVE

This positive, *wider* context of love for a person is key to understanding the Church's teaching on sexual morality. Joe, for example, truly wants to love his girlfriend as a person and not just as a source of pleasure. He chooses not to engage in sexual activity with her, understanding that sexual intercourse is meant to express total self-giving love.

A sexual expression of complete self-giving love makes sense within marriage, where husband and wife surrender themselves to each other completely in a lifelong commitment of love. Joe and his girlfriend, however, have not yet entered into such a relationship of full commitment and self-gift. A sexual relationship for them, therefore, would be a lie: Devoid of the total lifelong commitment to each other as persons and the complete self-giving love that comes in marriage, sexual intercourse in the end would be about using each other for the pleasure associated with this profound act of love. Therefore, choosing chastity helps free them from such pleasure-seeking utilitarianism and enables their relationship to develop, possibly, into a deeper self-giving love.

In short, chastity moderates our human desires for pleasure and allows us to experience a clear, pure love of the other person— a love that is truly centered on the other person's good, not just our own enjoyment. As John Paul II explains, "The word 'chaste' ('clean') implies liberation from everything that 'makes dirty'. Love must be so to speak pellucid: through all the sensations, all the actions which originate in it we must always be able to discern an attitude to a person of the opposite sex which derives from sincere affirmation of the worth of that person" (146).

> Chastity is *not* "one long no.'" Rather, it is a yes in our hearts to the other person.

The Difference between the Sixth and Ninth Commandments

One of the main fronts in the battle for purity is what John Paul II calls "sensual egoism," which is the tendency to use another person for sensual pleasure. Certainly, various sinful sexual acts constitute this kind of egoism. But John Paul II stresses that one can fall into sensual egoism without making any bodily contact with another person. For example, as we saw earlier, a man can view a woman primarily in terms of the value of her body. And he can use her body as an object of enjoyment whenever he sees her or even in his memory and imagination long after he has seen her (108).

The Ten Commandments reflect this point. The sixth commandment, on one hand, addresses external physical actions in the realm of sex: You shall not commit adultery. The ninth commandment, on the other hand, addresses internal actions commonly known as lustful thoughts: You shall not covet your neighbor's wife (147–148).

But it's not always easy to discern the boundary between simply noticing someone's sexual values and being attracted to them in a sinful way. What is the difference between an innocent interest in another person's physical appearance and a lustful thought? John Paul II offers some very helpful insights.

The pope identifies three general stages we experience in the battle against sensual egoism. In the first stage, one may experience a *spontaneous sensual reaction*. At this stage, one happens to notice the sexual values of another person's body and reacts to those values spontaneously. For example, a man walks into a cocktail party, catches the eye of a woman he has never met, notices the woman's attractive features, and finds himself drawn to her throughout the evening.

The sexual values of the opposite sex often present themselves spontaneously like this. We notice the sexual values and find ourselves interested in them. This is not lust, nor is it sinful. It simply means we are human and have human sensual desire. As John Paul II explains, sensuality "merely orients the whole psyche towards the sexual values, awakening an interest in or indeed an 'absorption' in them" (148). As we have seen previously, such sensual desire is given by God to draw persons together in love. This can lead to authentic love if the sensual attraction leads to a deeper level of commitment to the person, not just to the person's sexual values.

LUSTFUL THOUGHTS?

However, John Paul II warns us of how easy it is to move from the first stage of simple interest in the sexual values of another person to the second stage of hankering after them as a potential object of sensual pleasure. John Paul II calls this second stage *sensual concupiscence*. At this point, something within the person begins to stir: a desire for the sexual values of the other person's body *as an object to enjoy.*

Now the sexual values are not simply an object of interest, but an actual object of sensual desire in the heart. Something within us "begins to strive towards, to hanker after, that value" (148), and this reaction can culminate in "a desire to possess the value" (148).

Still, John Paul II says that even this second stage of sensual attraction is not necessarily sinful. It is the effect of concupiscence, our fallen inclination toward sin. Because of original sin, it is not easy for us to quickly direct that inner stirring of sensual desire to selfless love for the other person. Our desire for sensual pleasure is so powerful that we experience a desire to use the other person in order to gain that pleasure.

But here is the key: Even this stirring of sensual desire is not in itself sinful, John Paul II says, as long as the will *resists* that desire to use the person—as long as the will does not consent to it. Indeed, we may experience sensual desire mounting intensely within us without our will actually consenting to it and even with our will directly opposing it (162).

Don't Expect Immediate Victory

That is why John Paul II wisely reminds us that we cannot expect to win the battle for purity in our hearts immediately, simply by saying no hard enough. He says, "An act of will directed against a sensual impulse does not generally produce any immediate result. In its own (psychological) sphere a sensual reaction generally runs its full course even if it meets emphatic opposition in the sphere of the will. No-one can demand of himself either that he should experience no sensual reactions at all, or that they should immediately yield just because the will does not consent, or even because it declares itself definitely 'against'"(162).

This is very helpful advice for anyone desiring, but struggling, to be chaste. One might try with all his might to remain pure but still experience simple, spontaneous, sensual reactions and even the inner stirrings of concupiscent desires. Yet one must remember that *as long as the will does not consent to those utilitarian desires, he or she has not fallen into sin.* As John Paul II makes clear, "There is a difference between 'not wanting' and 'not feeling', 'not experiencing'" (162).

"I thought it was cool to hook up with as many people as possible because that's how dating was modeled for me in all the movies."

In other words, one may feel the inner stirring of concupiscent desire, but this is not the same as giving the will consent to follow those desires and treat the other person as a potential object of enjoyment. John Paul II explains:

> a sensual reaction, or the "stirring of" carnal desire which results from it, and which occurs irrespectively and independently of the will, cannot in themselves be sins. No, we must give proper weight to the fact that *in any normal man the lust of the body has its own dynamic*, of which his sensual reactions are a manifestation. We have drawn attention to their appetitive character. The sexual values connected with the body of the person become not only an object of interest but—quite easily—the object of sensual desire. The source of this desire is the power of concupiscence (*appetitus concupiscibilis* as St. Thomas calls it), and so not the will (161).

CROSSING THE THRESHOLD OF SIN

Nevertheless, we must be on guard and strongly strive against these concupiscent sensual desires. Left unchecked, they continually try to get the will to consent to them, thereby leading the person to cross the line of sin. Indeed, if the will does not resist this stirring of the sensual appetite, a person falls into the third stage, which John Paul II calls *carnal desire.*

Here, the will gives up resisting, throws in the towel, and consents to pursuing the pleasurable feelings occurring within. The man (or woman) deliberately commits the will to the promptings of the body, even though those promptings direct him to treat the other's body as an object of enjoyment whether in thought, memory, or imagination or in actual external sexual actions.

Take, for example, a man who was struggling for purity but then consents to look at a woman lustfully. "As soon as the will consents it begins actively to want what is spontaneously 'happening' in the senses and the sensual appetites. From then onwards, this is not something merely 'happening' to a man, but something which he himself begins actively doing" (162).

Now the threshold of sin has been crossed. Before this point, the man had maintained an important level of purity in his heart because he was resisting those utilitarian concupiscent desires. But now that his will consents to those desires, something dramatic changes: The man himself changes as he wills in his heart to go along with those utilitarian desires. He is no longer simply experiencing a desire to use the woman's body; he actually is using her body as an outlet for his carnal desire.

He is no longer simply a man struggling against lustful thoughts; he has become a lustful man who has consented to those thoughts in which he is exploiting the woman's body for his own pleasure in his imagination.

LUSTFUL THOUGHTS?

Crossing the Threshold of Sin

Stage One Spontaneous Sensual Reaction	*Stage Two* Sensual Desire (sensual concupiscence)	*Stage Three* Carnal Desire (carnal concupiscence)
Simple, spontaneous interest in sexual values	Desire for the sexual values as an object for pleasure begins to stir within the person	The will gives up resisting and consents to pursue this desire
	But the will has not consented, is trying to resist this desire	The deliberate commitment of the will to use the body as an object for pleasure whether in the memory and imagination (lustful thoughts) or in external sexual actions (lustful acts)
Not sinful, but may be a near occasion of sin	Not sinful, but dangerous	Sinful
	Will must resist and not consent	

WHAT DO YOU DO WHEN YOU MEET BATHSHEBA?

The biblical account of how David fell into adultery with Bathsheba sheds light on these stages of sensuality (2 Samuel 11:1–5). One day, David arose, looked out his balcony, and happened to see a woman bathing on a rooftop below. He immediately noticed that this woman was beautiful. David did not plan this encounter or seek this woman out. The sexual values of this woman's body suddenly and unexpectedly appeared before him, and he couldn't help but notice them and be interested in them. This alone was not sinful. David noticing her body simply indicates that he was a normal human being attracted to the sexual values of the opposite sex.

What should David have done when he saw the beautiful woman bathing? He should have turned away immediately in order to prevent himself from falling into the deeper, more intense levels of sensual desire. But David didn't turn his eyes away and remove himself from the situation. Instead, he gazed at her and wondered about her. He let his curiosity get the best of him. He even called his servants to the balcony to ask them who she was.

At this stage, David seems to have been moving from an innocent spontaneous sensual response to the craving of sensual desire. And this is what got David into trouble. In the end, David failed to resist his sensual desires and deliberately did something to feed them. After his servants told him the woman was Bathsheba, the wife of Uriah the Hittite, David decided to act on his impulses and thus fell into sinful carnal desire. He called Bathsheba over to his palace and committed adultery with her.

This ancient biblical story has much application for our lives today. Beautiful women's bodies still suddenly appear before the eyes of godly men even when they are not looking for such sensual stimulation. A man can be walking down the street and notice a woman with a short skirt who arrests his attention. He can be driving down the highway and be faced with a provocatively dressed woman on a billboard. He can be watching a football game when suddenly at the commercial break, half-naked women start running around promoting beer and cars.

And although men are more immediately affected by such visual stimuli, many women today find themselves fighting a similar battle, tempted by the deliberately provocative images of men that are common in our highly sexualized culture. They, too, are at risk of falling into sinful carnal desires. Especially in an age of magazines like *Cosmo*, and online pornography, many young women are growing up more sexualized than ever before.

Therefore, for both men and women, temptation may appear out of the blue in many forms. The key question is, "What will we do when these moments happen?" Will we immediately turn away before the stirring of sensual desire takes over? Or will we be like David and feed our curiosity? The story of David reminds us of the importance of extinguishing impure thoughts and glances right from the very beginning, before the fire of sensuality goes ablaze.

We Become What We Watch

This also sheds light on why we should be very careful about what we take in from the media. Everywhere we turn in our culture, we are bombarded with shows, movies, songs, and images that that have a sexualized view of love. Instead of being an expression of total self-giving love in marriage, sex is portrayed as a pleasurable recreational sport that everyone should enjoy if they have feelings for each other. "All the people in the movies who are having the awesome dating relationships are having sex. Maybe I should be willing to have sex, too, because that's what all the beautiful stories show us," one young adult said.

Even many good Christians have admitted how the love stories from Hollywood affect them. They might know in their heads that they should wait to be married, but in their hearts, they begin to wonder if it's OK. It also has an impact on the way they approach relationships with the opposite sex. "I grew up Catholic, went to church,

> "I didn't really want to date this guy, but I felt good about myself knowing he was interested in me: I'm being pursued, I'm wanted, I'm interesting."

and went to youth group. But I thought it was cool to hook up with as many people as possible because that's how dating was modeled for me in all the movies. I just imitated what I saw the cool guys doing."

EMOTIONAL CHASTITY

One final reflection: Perhaps the lessons John Paul II offers on the stages of sensual desire can be applied somewhat analogously to emotional attractions as well. A man may encounter a woman who has a warm personality and find himself instantly experiencing an emotional attraction to her. He didn't do anything to seek this out; it just happened. This is a spontaneous emotional reaction to the woman's femininity. However, just as we saw with sensual reactions, what one chooses to do with this initial sentimental attraction is crucial.

Take, for example, a single woman who finds herself spending much of her time daydreaming about a certain man she hopes will notice her. Such a premature emotional attachment could distract her from her responsibilities at work or school, from her family and friendships, and even from her relationship with God, as much of her time in prayer is spent thinking of that man.

Similarly, a married man could find himself growing emotionally attached to a woman who is not his wife. If he finds himself thinking about this other woman throughout the day, wanting to see her, and worried about what she thinks of him, it is a clear sign that his heart is divided and not fully united to his wife's.

This even applies to religious sisters who have made a vow to Jesus Christ as their spouse. A sister would not be giving her whole heart to Christ if she were allowing herself to think a lot about a certain man and seek his attention and affirmation for the good feelings she experiences from him.

We also can use people for the attention we receive from them, leading them on without having any desire for a relationship. Some single women, for example, have admitted, "I've used guys to overcome my fear of being alone. It's just nice to have someone interested in me!" Or, "I didn't really want to date this guy, but I felt good about myself knowing he was interested in me—I'm being pursued, I'm wanted, I'm interesting. But looking back, it was selfish. I was just using him to meet my emotional needs."

Guarding the Heart

This initial experience of various emotional attractions is in itself not sinful. If I am married to someone else, however, or if I am a priest or religious, these initial emotional attractions can become particularly dangerous if I'm not careful. In these cases, the vital question I must face is, "What will I do with these sentiments?"

There are two options. I can choose to treat these feelings like impure thoughts and strive to prevent the emotional attraction from spinning out of control by turning away. I could curtail conversations with the person I'm attracted to, for example, or perhaps avoid spending time with the person. To be sure, some serious situations call for a complete break from any contact since this may be the only way to free one's heart from the inappropriate emotional attachment.

Or, I can choose to give in to the sentimental attraction and feed it even though I'm married to someone else. In social settings, I can allow myself to gravitate toward conversation with this particular person. Throughout the day, I can let myself think about this person and dream about some imaginary life together. I can permit myself to go out of my way to see this person and talk to him or her. I may even open my heart to this individual, sharing personal details about my life and seeking to be emotionally fulfilled by the person's interest in me.

In Christian circles, improper relationships like this may disguise themselves as spiritual: I pray for this other person, and we share intimate details about our spiritual lives. Yet when I begin to form an emotional attachment to someone of the opposite sex to whom I am not married, I am falling into a kind of infidelity. Even though I may not be committing adultery in the body, I am giving my heart to someone who is not my spouse.

Christ, however, wants us to live single-heartedly. He wants our hearts to be completely united to him and to our spouse. Only the person who is able to guard his heart, reserving it for his spouse, is able to live out his vocation faithfully and love his spouse with total self-giving love.

For Further Reading
Love and Responsibility, pp. 159–173

For Discussion and Reflection

1. Do people tend to view chastity as something restrictive or something freeing? Why? Why do you think John Paul II says chastity is foremost a yes rather than "one long 'no'"?

2. How can understanding the three stages in the battle against sensual egoism help one resist lustful thoughts and actions? What helpful insights did you gain from John Paul II's explanation of these stages?

3. Living chastity, interiorly and exteriorly, can be a great struggle. John Paul II reminds us that having self-control in other areas of our lives can help us in the battle for purity: "*Moderation is not mediocrity but the ability to maintain one's equilibrium amid the stirrings of concupiscence*" (196). He concludes, "whoever is not self-controlled and moderate is not chaste" (196). What are some positive ways we can practice moderation and self-control in other areas of our lives so that we can have the virtue to resist those particular temptations against purity that may come our way?

4. Consider the following quote from St. Francis de Sales: "[Chastity] may be lost both by the body's external senses and by thoughts and desires within the heart.... I recall to your mind an expression that an ancient father, John Cassian, relates as coming from the mouth of the great St. Basil. Speaking of himself, he said one day, 'I have not known women, yet I am not a virgin.'" [1]

   Even many great saints struggled to overcome impurity— and by God's grace, they triumphed. How can you strive to keep not only your body but also your mind and heart pure?

5. Reflect on this verse: "Finally, brethren, whatever is true, whatever is honorable, whatever is just, whatever is pure, whatever is lovely, whatever is gracious, if there is any excellence, if there is anything worthy of praise, think about these things" (Philippians 4:8). How can we put this verse into practice in our own lives? How can living the ideal in this verse help us in the battle for purity?

6. While some Christians make a strong effort to guard their *physical* purity in their relationships with the opposite sex, not all make it a priority to guard their heart. Yet John Paul II warns of the dangers of what he calls an "emotional egoism," which is the tendency to use another person for emotional pleasure. What are some examples of emotional egoism? How can these become a threat to love? How should men and women guard their hearts?

chapter nine

To Inspire Love: A Return to Modesty

Does it really matter what kind of clothing a woman chooses to wear?

Skimpy dresses, miniskirts, tiny bikinis, low-rise pants, and cutout shirts have become mainstream attire for young women in today's post-sexual-revolution world. Anyone who might raise questions about the appropriateness of such dress is viewed as rigid or out of touch with modern style. Modesty is no longer a part of our culture's vocabulary. Though most people sense they wouldn't want their own daughters dressing like the latest pop stars, few have the courage to bring up the topic of modesty, and even fewer would know what to say if they did.

John Paul II, however, offers much needed wisdom on the nature of modesty and how dressing modestly is crucial for strengthening our relationships with the opposite sex.

SHAME

John Paul II begins his treatment on modesty with an explanation of a common human experience: shame. Shame involves a tendency to conceal something—not just bad things, such as sins, weaknesses, and embarrassing moments, but also good things that we want to keep from coming out in the open. Someone who performs a good deed may prefer that his action go unnoticed, for example. He may feel embarrassed if he receives a public compliment, not because he did something bad but because he doesn't want to draw attention to his deed.

Similarly, a student who receives high marks on an exam may feel embarrassed when the teacher praises her in front of the class, because she wanted to share her good grade only with her closest friends and family. There are many good things that we wish to keep hidden from public eyes, and we feel shame if they are brought out into the open.

Immodest dress might attract men to lust after her body, but it won't inspire men to love her as a person.

This helps us understand one of the most powerful experiences of shame: *sexual* shame. Why do human persons tend to conceal body parts associated with sexuality? Why do men and women instinctively cover themselves quickly if someone of the opposite sex accidentally walks in on them while they are changing their clothes? John Paul II explains that this tendency to conceal those parts of the body that make it male or female is itself not the essence of shame. Rather, it is a manifestation of a deeper tendency "to conceal the sexual values themselves, particularly in so far as they constitute in the mind of a particular person 'a potential object of enjoyment' for persons of the other sex" (176).

For example, a woman may instinctively sense that if certain parts of her body are exposed, a man might view her merely for her sexual values, as an object of pleasure. And those particular parts of her body reveal her sexual values so powerfully that indeed a man can be drawn primarily to those sexual values and not to her value as a person.

That is why we tend to veil the sexual values connected with particular parts of the body—not because they are bad, but because they can overshadow the greater value of the person. John Paul II says sexual shame is "a natural *form of self-defense for the person*" (182). It helps prevent the person from being treated as an object of enjoyment.

Thus, the concealing of sexual values through modesty of dress is meant to provide the arena in which something much more than a sensual reaction might take place. Modesty of dress helps protect interactions between the sexes from falling into utilitarianism and thus creates the possibility for authentic love to develop.

SHAME ABSORBED BY LOVE

Yet within the context of betrothed love—a mature self-giving love of a husband and wife—there is no longer any reason for shame. True love makes certain that sentimental and sensual experiences "are imbued with affirmation of the value of the person to such an extent that it is impossible for the will to regard the other person as an object for use" (183–184). Each person has confidence in the other's selfless love. They each have trust that they won't be treated merely as an object for the other person's pleasure. Hence, their emotional and sensual enjoyment is grounded in full self-giving love and a profound sense of responsibility for the other person.

> The need for shame has been absorbed by mature love for a person: it is no longer necessary for a lover to conceal from the beloved or from himself a disposition to enjoy, since this has been absorbed by true love ruled by the will. Affirmation of the value of the person so thoroughly permeates all the sensual and emotional reactions connected with the sexual values that the will is not threatened by a utilitarian outlook (184).

This kind of trust, however, can only be found fully in betrothed love. Only in a healthy, thriving marriage is shame absorbed by love in this way. That's why we want to dress modestly when we are with a member of the opposite sex to whom we are not married. Outside the context of betrothed love, we must be careful with the unveiling of sexual values or else we will set ourselves up to be used by the opposite sex.

MODESTY: FROM THE WOMAN'S PERSPECTIVE

This helps make sense out of why women should want to dress modestly. Unfortunately, some discussions on modesty today tend to be negative and legalistic—rules about what a woman shouldn't wear and lessons about how immodest dress leads men into lustful thoughts. As a result, modesty is often seen merely as something that women are obliged to do for the sake of helping lustful men avoid the near occasion of sin.

A true story might help illustrate this point. A woman attended Mass wearing immodest clothing. When the Mass was over, a young man confronted her on her choice in pants and blamed her for the impure thoughts he had during the liturgy: "I was sitting behind you today, and I want you to know that because you were wearing tight jeans, I fell into lustful thoughts during Mass and couldn't receive Communion today."

It might be true that this particular woman should have been more careful about the kind of clothes she was wearing, especially to Mass. But she can't be blamed entirely for that man's lustful thoughts. In the end, he is responsible for his own actions.

While one important benefit of modest dress is that it helps prevent men from falling into sin, this is not the whole story. John Paul II helps us to see that modesty is first and foremost something positive and very good for the woman herself. Modesty not only protects women from being treated as objects, it also inspires men to respond to them with the kind of authentic, selfless love that every woman longs for in her heart.

THREE PATHS TO MODESTY

Now we are prepared to explore the three aspects of sexual shame presented by John Paul II and consider how they relate to modesty. We have already touched on the first aspect: that shame tends to conceal sexual values so they don't produce merely a sexual reaction in another person. A woman should want to avoid dressing in a way that deliberately draws attention to

> Modesty seeks to inspire love—true love for the person, not just a sexual reaction to a woman's body.

her sexual values to such an extent that it obscures her value as a person.

Nevertheless, some women may object: "If a man struggles with lustful thoughts, that's *his* problem, not mine. Why do I need to dress modestly?" But this objection misses John Paul II's point. Remember, the purpose of modesty is not merely to help prevent men from stumbling into impure thoughts. Modesty of dress is primarily meant to protect *the woman* herself.

John Paul II offers two important insights that help make sense of this. First, we must remember that human beings are fallen. It is not easy for us to avoid a utilitarian attitude when we see the body of the opposite sex. Simply saying, "I shouldn't have to worry about how I dress" naively fails to take this effect of original sin seriously.

As John Paul II notes, *"Man, alas, is not such a perfect being that the sight of the body of another person, especially a person of the other sex, can arouse in him merely a disinterested liking which develops into an innocent affection.* In practice it also arouses concupiscence, or a wish to enjoy concentrated on sexual values with no regard for the value of the person" (190). He further explains that, as a result of original sin, a man "too easily accepts the sensual reaction and reduces another person, because of the person's 'body and sex', to the role of an object for enjoyment" (191).

When this happens, John Paul II calls it *"depersonalization by sexualization"* (191). Modesty of dress, therefore, is in the woman's best interest. It helps protect her from being treated by fallen men as an object for exploitation.

Second, John Paul II also reminds us that men struggle with sensuality in a way that is difficult for women to understand, since sensuality is more powerful in a man than it is in a woman. Because of this, women have an even greater need to conceal from men the sexual values of their body. This is difficult for women to appreciate since they don't experience sensuality in this way.

As John Paul II explains, "For since a woman does not find in herself the sensuality of which a man as a rule cannot but be aware in himself she does not feel so great a need to conceal 'the body as a potential object of enjoyment'" (177). This helps explain why some young women, when they first hear about modesty, are shocked at how men might view them if they wear certain kinds of shirts, blouses, skirts, or pants. They might have absolutely no idea that the way they are dressing might be inviting men to view them as an object.

John Paul II points out that "very often, a woman does not regard a particular way of dressing as shameless (we are speaking here of 'physical shamelessness'), although some man, or indeed many men, may find it so" (189). However, keeping in mind this crucial difference between men and women—that men have a powerful sensual desire that women themselves do not experience—can help women better understand what actually constitutes modesty and better appreciate the need to dress in a way that protects them from being used.

CONCEALING OUR REACTIONS

The second aspect of sexual shame is its tendency to conceal our own utilitarian reactions to the opposite sex when we treat them as objects for our enjoyment. We realize that a human person is not an object for use, and we feel ashamed if we treat people that way in our glances, thoughts, or imagination. Deep down, a man senses, "'I must not touch her, not even with a deeply hidden wish to enjoy her, for she cannot be an object for use'" (180).

Consider what often happens when a man is staring at a woman lustfully and she notices it. As soon as he is caught, he quickly turns his eyes away because he *feels ashamed* of what he was doing. He does not want his utilitarian attitude toward her to be exposed. Deep down, he knows that he shouldn't treat a woman that way and that the woman feels uncomfortable with his utilitarian looks, so he immediately looks away.

This is what makes a man who shamelessly stares down a woman so pathetic. At least the lustful man who turns his eyes away has some sense of shame in what he's doing. But the man who continues to look at the woman lustfully, even if she notices, has no shame whatsoever. He is openly lusting after her and does not care.

INSPIRING LOVE

The third and most important aspect of sexual shame is its connection with love. Ultimately, modesty seeks to inspire love—true love for the person, not just a sexual reaction to a woman's body. Deep in a woman's heart is a longing to inspire and experience love. Thus, a woman should dress in a way that inspires love for her as a person. Dressing immodestly, however, hinders the possibilities for true love to develop, for it draws attention to her sexual values to such an extent that it overshadows her value as a person.

A woman who dresses provocatively may indeed gain attention from men. However, she must ask whether this is really the kind of attention she wants to receive. Immodest dress might attract men to lust after her body as an object of enjoyment, but it won't inspire men to love her as a person.

Modesty of dress is about so much more than helping men avoid falling into sin. And it is not simply a "defensive reflex" protecting women from being used. In the end, as John Paul II explains, "sexual modesty is not a flight from love, but on the contrary the opening of a way towards it. *The spontaneous need to conceal mere sexual values bound up with the person is the natural way to the discovery of the value of the person as such*" (179).

Bathing Suits and Hospital Gowns

At the end of his chapter on shame and modesty, John Paul II mentions certain situations in which partial or total nudity would not be considered immodest. The body may be partially uncovered for certain functional purposes such as physical labor, a medical examination, or bathing. That same attire which may be modest within its functional setting, however, can become immodest when taken out of that particular context.

He gives the example of a bathing suit. A modest bathing suit may be appropriate for a woman at the pool, but the same outfit

becomes very immodest if she wears it into the office for work, out
to dinner at a restaurant, or out for a walk in the park (191–192).

THE WARDROBE DILEMMA

We will conclude with a few application points. Many young
women who become convinced about the importance of modesty
face very practical issues when they turn to their wardrobes.
"Should I wear this dress?" "How do I know if this piece of
clothing is truly modest or
not?" There are many guidelines for modest dress, but we
will consider only three points
in this chapter.

> "If you are practically naked in
> front of people you hardly know,
> your self-consciousness might be
> your natural thermometer telling
> you that something is off."
> –Wendy Shalit

First, most women have at
least a basic level of intuition
about modesty, even if it has
been obscured by the prevailing culture. Young women might
wear certain types of clothing items because they are in fashion
but still feel somewhat ill at ease doing so. That uncomfortable
feeling may be the woman's intuition trying to tell her that something is not quite right in the way she is dressing.

My wife, for example, told me of a young, devout Catholic
woman she saw at a conference who looked intensely uncomfortable with the clothes she was wearing. She constantly pulled
down her skirt whenever she sat. Throughout the day, she felt the
need to cover her arms and chest more and to pull up her blouse
every time she leaned over. She seemed to know instinctively that
too much of her body was being exposed. This is a positive sign,
for it seems to indicate that at least some women possess a good
internal gauge for discerning whether certain attire is immodest: If
a woman constantly feels she needs to readjust her outfit in order

to cover her skin or block certain views of her body, it's probably a sign that she doesn't have enough clothes on!

As Wendy Shalit put it in her book, *A Return to Modesty*, "If you are practically naked in front of people you hardly know, your self-consciousness might be your natural thermometer telling you that something is off."[1]

Second, a woman may want to ask trustworthy, virtuous men or older female friends for their thoughts about modesty and for feedback on particular clothing items. My wife and I have had college women seek our counsel about matters of modesty and about particular clothes they were considering wearing for dances and other social events. I know groups of young women who have met to look at clothing catalogues and discuss how to relate principles of modesty to today's fashions. An outside perspective can be helpful, especially from people who have thought through the issue before and applied it to today's culture.

Third, a woman in our society needs to be bold when it comes to modesty. John Paul II is not saying women must dress like they're from the Victorian age, but he does want them to be careful. Dress can accentuate sexual values in certain circumstances, he says, but we must be very careful not to wear clothing that draws too much attention to the sexual values and ends up obscuring the value of the person (190).

Much of the mainstream fashion trends, however, make it very difficult for a woman to find modest clothing and still be in style. This is especially evident in the challenges some Catholic women face in finding modest wedding dresses. I know of women who spent countless hours searching online and in the stores for a dress that is elegant and yet doesn't draw too much attention to their flesh on the most important day of their lives. But working hard to find a modest wedding dress is well worth the effort: I also know of women who deeply regret what they wore on their wedding day, so much so that they are embarrassed to show their own friends and children their wedding pictures.

In conclusion, John Paul II reminds us that what we wear does make a difference in our relationships with the opposite sex. While much more could be said about the specifics regarding what constitutes modest or immodest dress, John Paul II provides fundamental principles on modesty that we can apply to varied situations. Even more, his chapter on shame and modesty in *Love and Responsibility* encourages us to renew the conversation on the forgotten virtue of modesty and gives us a beginning framework for that discussion.

FOR FURTHER READING
Love and Responsibility, pp. 174–193

FOR DISCUSSION AND REFLECTION

1. What are your initial thoughts or reactions when you hear the word *modesty*? How do our culture and the media typically portray modesty? What are some of the challenges people face in embracing modesty within our secularized society?

2. How would you explain what John Paul II means when he speaks of shame in general? What is *sexual* shame in particular? How do his reflections on shame shed light on this common human experience?

3. How do you think modesty benefits women? How does it benefit men? And finally, how does modesty benefit relationships between women and men?

4. John Paul II says modesty is something women generally will have a difficult time understanding. What does he mean by this? Do you think this is true? Explain.

5. What does it mean to dress and act in a way that "inspires love"?

6. What are some practical guidelines you can set for yourself to embrace John Paul II's unique and positive vision of modesty?

7. John Paul II writes, "What is truly immodest in dress is that which frankly contributes to the deliberate displacement of the true value of the person by sexual values, that which is bound to elicit a reaction to the person as to a 'possible means of obtaining sexual enjoyment'" (190). How do mainstream styles today relate to modesty? What are some examples of popular fashions that are not modest?

8. The *Catechism of the Catholic Church* states:

> Modesty protects the intimate center of the person. It means refusing to unveil what should remain hidden. It is ordered to chastity to whose sensitivity it bears witness. It guides how one looks at others and behaves toward them in conformity with the dignity of persons and their solidarity.
>
> Modesty protects the mystery of persons and their love. It encourages patience and moderation in loving relationships; it requires that the conditions for the definitive giving and commitment of man and woman to one another be fulfilled. Modesty is decency. It inspires one's choice of clothing. It keeps silence or reserve where there is evident risk of unhealthy curiosity. It is discreet.
>
> There is a modesty of the feelings as well as of the body.... [M]odesty exists as an intuition of the spiritual dignity proper to man. (2521–2524)

How does modesty include far more than a choice of clothing? How can we allow modesty to permeate all aspects of our lives, ultimately preserving the mystery and dignity of persons and their love?

chapter ten

Men, Women, and Tenderness

*H*olding hands, an embrace, a kiss—these can be innocent expressions of love. But without great vigilance and virtue, these outward expressions can easily become a form of utilitarianism that actually ends up driving two people farther apart and preventing love from fully developing.

This is a point John Paul II makes when he addresses the topic of tenderness. He explains that the essence of tenderness is found "in the tendency to make one's own the feelings and mental states of another person" (201). This is a common experience in romantic relationships, as men and women feel closely involved with the inner life of their beloved, entering into the other person's feelings and state of mind.

Tenderness also seeks outward expression. It's not enough to have an awareness of what is going on inside the other person. One also wants to communicate that sense of closeness to his beloved. "I feel the need to let the other 'I' know that I take his feelings and his state of mind to heart, to make this other human being feel that I am sharing it all, that I am feeling what he feels" (201–202). We thus express this tenderness through various outward actions—holding a person to one's chest, putting one's arms around the other, kissing the other person.

PREMATURE TENDERNESS

Tenderness may be quite selfless and innocent when it is based on concern for another person and what that person is going through interiorly. However, John Paul II warns that outward gestures such as an embrace or a kiss can lose their altruistic character and quickly fall into utilitarianism if they are used primarily as a means to one's own pleasure. Once "the need to gratify one's own feelings" begins to overshadow genuine selfless concern for the other, expressions of tenderness have crossed over into egoism and will prevent love from fully developing (203).

> Premature acts of tenderness create only an illusion of love.

And crossing that line into egoism is something we can easily fall into, for two reasons. First, as John Paul II reminds us, the love between men and women is driven in large part by sensuality and sentimentality, which are never fully satisfied and are constantly demanding ever greater amounts of pleasure. Given our fallen human nature, outward expressions of tenderness may be sought more for the emotional or sensual pleasure we receive than for a selfless desire to enter into the inner life of the other person. "Hence, various forms of tenderness can easily diverge from love of the person, and stray in the direction of sensual, or at any rate emotional, egoism" (205).

Second, as we have seen, the subjective aspects of love, the powerful emotions or sensual pleasure we experience, develop more quickly than the objective aspects of virtue, such as friendship, self-giving, and responsibility. Since the emotion of love is for many people experienced as "a sudden and powerful explosion," many are tempted to give or receive outward expressions of tenderness before those objective aspects of love have had a chance to develop (205). And as we've seen in previous reflections, those objective aspects are crucial to ensure that the relationship remains at the level of self-giving love and does not fall into utilitarianism. That's why premature acts of tenderness are very harmful to love, for they create only "an illusion of love, a love which in reality does not exist" (205).

Indeed, when we give or receive an embrace, a kiss, or some other expression of tenderness prematurely before the objective elements of love have matured—we are actually putting up roadblocks to love. The pope explains:

> Accordingly, if we are to grant a man or a woman the 'right to tenderness'—whether to show it, or to receive it—we must also demand a greater sense of responsibility. There undoubtedly exists a tendency, more pronounced in some than in others, to enlarge those rights, to seek to enjoy them prematurely when both are only at the stage of the arousal of sentiment, and with it of sensuality, while the objective aspect of love, and the union of persons, are still missing. Such premature tenderness in the association of a man and a woman quite often even destroys love, or at least prevents it from developing fully, of ripening both internally and objectively into a genuine love. (205–206)

Going Too Far?

The experience of many young people bears this out. In the early stages of a relationship, a man and woman may begin to develop a good friendship. They may spend a lot of time going for walks, going out for coffee, socializing in larger groups of people—always in good conversation with each other, getting to know each other. But once the relationship becomes physical, those physical forms of intimacy increasingly become more central to the relationship, while real communication, working through problems, and growing in virtue together gradually slide.

And that should not surprise us. Once we experience the powerful feelings associated with sensual pleasure prematurely, it's no wonder we are less likely to cultivate the objective aspects of love that require more work. Why go through all that effort when the sensual pleasures can be so easily and immediately obtained? In reality, however, the giving or receiving of premature tenderness creates only the appearance of love, and it often covers up the real underlying attitude driving a relationship: an egoism, a selfishness, that is the very opposite of love.

That's why we must be extremely careful in giving or receiving acts of tenderness. John Paul II says expressions of tenderness should always be accompanied by an even greater sense of responsibility for the other person.

> There can be no genuine tenderness without a perfected habit of continence, which has its origin in a will always ready to show loving kindness, and so overcome the temptation merely to enjoy put in its way by sensuality and carnal concupiscence. Without such continence, the natural energies of sensuality, and the energies of sentiment drawn into their orbit, will become merely the "raw material" of sensual or at best emotional egoism (207).

THE TREMORS OF MARRIAGE

After treating the dangers of premature tenderness, which applies especially to dating and courtship relationships, John Paul II goes on to discuss the crucial positive role tenderness must play in marriage. He discusses not just the outward manifestations of tenderness, but more fundamentally, tenderness itself.

In marriage, tenderness should involve "the steady participation of emotion, of a durable commitment to love, for it is this that brings a man and a woman close together, creates an interior climate of 'communicativeness'" (206). He then says that "a great deal" of this kind of tenderness is needed in a marriage.

In this context, John Paul II offers a second, even fuller definition of tenderness, in light of how it applies to the spousal relationship: *"Tenderness is the ability to feel with and for the whole person, to feel even the most deeply hidden spiritual tremors, and always to have in mind the true good of that person"* (207). What a powerful description! To feel "the most deeply hidden spiritual tremors." Do you feel what is going on most deeply in the soul of your spouse? Her hopes, his fears, her burdens, his wounds?

> Do you feel what is going on most deeply in the soul of your spouse?

The pope challenges spouses to have hearts that are truly united, truly able to enter into the inner lives of one another. He writes, "tenderness creates a feeling of not being alone, a feeling that her or his whole life is equally the content of another and very dear person's life. This conviction very greatly facilitates and reinforces their sense of unity" (207).

WIVES AND TENDERNESS

Finally, John Paul II says women not only expect this type of tenderness from their husbands, but that they actually have a special right to it in marriage. He gives three reasons for why husbands need to enter deeply into the emotional lives of their wives.

First, at the most basic level, the woman's emotional life is generally deeper than a man's. The woman, therefore, has a greater need for tenderness, even though men may have a difficult time understanding this since they don't share that need as much. Just as women may not fully grasp the power of sensuality in a man—and therefore struggle with modesty—so men may have difficulty appreciating the depth of their wives' emotional sphere—and may fail to show them the tenderness they need.

A woman has a greater need for her husband to enter into her emotional sphere and the depths of her inner life.

Yet, being aware of the woman's richer emotional life can make a big difference in a marriage. In fact, popular marriage books today emphasize this point. Women typically need more time to talk than men, tend to be more relational, and generally don't want their husbands to solve their problems as much as they want their husbands to listen to and understand them. In short, a woman has a greater need for her husband to enter into her emotional sphere and the depths of her inner life.

Second, the woman *gives herself* to a man. Since women generally have a much richer emotional life, when they marry, they might feel the break with parents and family more acutely than men, especially if they come from a close-knit family and a strong relationship with their parents.

While most men look forward to starting the new adventure of marriage and building a life together with their wives, some women, while experiencing this excitement, also experience a sense of loss as they leave the people they have been most emotionally invested in to join themselves to their husbands. A woman has an even greater need for her husband to enter into her feelings and state of mind as she goes through this transition and surrenders herself in marriage to him.

Third, the woman goes through extremely important and difficult experiences in her life, which may include pregnancy, childbirth, nursing, caring for a newborn, leaving a job, and staying at home. Some women feel very alone in the midst of these new experiences. Thus, they have a special need for tenderness from their husbands as they go through these transitions.

THE CHALLENGE TO HUSBANDS

John Paul II challenges men to do much more than provide for their wives financially or take care of things around the house. He challenges husbands to enter deeply into their wives' emotional lives—*"to feel with and for the whole person"* (207). Men who get so caught up in work, sports, the nightly news, or projects at home while remaining emotionally distant from their own wives fail to provide the kind of tenderness he is describing, the kind of tenderness that women have a special right to in marriage.

This challenge to men is especially important when their wives become mothers, for that is perhaps when women need the tenderness of their husbands most. While motherhood is a great blessing, it is also physically and emotionally draining. Furthermore, our culture does not fully recognize the dignity and value of motherhood. Men in the workplace constantly earn praise, respect, and recognition for their professional accomplishments, but mothers who choose to stay at home and dedicate their lives full-time to raising children rarely receive such affirmation from the world. In fact, many times they are looked down upon.

In my own life, for example, people sometimes thank me for my books, articles, and teaching. But few people outside of our home go out of their way to thank my wife for giving her life to our children, whether it be for spiritual matters such as teaching them about Jesus and forming them in virtue or for the more mundane things like changing diapers, filling sippy cups, and reading *The Very Hungry Caterpillar* five times a day. Doing the Catholic apostolic work of writing and teaching can be a good thing, but it pales in comparison to what my wife does at home as she strives to give her whole life to raising our children for the glory of God.

In a culture that constantly affirms people for their productivity and accomplishments outside of the home and puzzlingly looks down on a woman who would choose to stay at home to raise children, it's no wonder many mothers feel very alone and second-guess their state in life as they transition from the workplace to motherhood. Men, more than ever before, need to go out of their way to support their wives and enter into the many "spiritual tremors" they encounter through these important events in their lives.

FOR FURTHER READING
Love and Responsibility, pp. 194–208

FOR DISCUSSION AND REFLECTION

1. What does John Paul II mean by the word *tenderness*? What role does tenderness play in a relationship?
2. What is the difference between tenderness itself and the outward expressions of tenderness? (See pp. 108–109 for more on this).
3. How might premature tenderness create an "illusion of love" in a relationship? What will likely be the outcome of a relationship that indulges in premature tenderness? What can we learn from John Paul II's discussion of this topic?
4. What are some practical ways people in dating, courtship, or engagement relationships can ensure that the outward

expressions of tenderness do not harm the relationship and hinder the opportunity for love to develop?

5. Tenderness in marriage: John Paul II defines tenderness as *"the ability to feel with and for the whole person,* to feel even the most deeply hidden spiritual tremors, and always to have in mind the true good of that person" (207). Have you ever witnessed a marital relationship where true tenderness was evident or one where it was obviously missing? What were the notable differences between these relationships? How do you think tenderness can facilitate and reinforce spousal unity?

6. While he was the bishop of Krakow, Karol Wojtyla wrote a beautiful play entitled *The Jeweler's Shop.* It focuses on three different couples and their relationships. In one scene, Anna speaks of her relationship with her husband, Stefan, which after many years, has grown cold and distant:

> Outwardly nothing changed.
> Stefan seemed to behave the same,
> but he could not heal the wound
> that had opened in my soul.
> It did not hurt him,
> he did not feel it.
> Maybe he did not want to.
> ...
> He left me with a hidden wound,
> thinking, no doubt, She will get over it.
> Besides, he was confident of his rights [to marital intercourse],
> whereas I wanted him to win them continually.
> I did not want to feel like an object
> that cannot be lost once it has been acquired.

...
Life changed
into a more and more strenuous existence of two people
who occupied
less and less room in each other.
Only the sum of duties remained,
a sum total conventional and changing,
removed further and further away
from the taste of enthusiasm.

...
Whether he was unfaithful to me I do not know,
since I took no interest in his life either.
He was indifferent to me.
I suppose after office hours he went to play cards,
and after drinking he would come home quite late,
without saying a word, or with some casual remark,
to which as a rule I responded with silence.[1]

How can a lack of real tenderness gradually destroy what may have once been a genuine betrothed love? What are some different ways spouses can preserve tenderness within their marriage, even over many years?

7. John Paul II says women have a special right to tenderness in marriage. Why is this so?

8. What do you think tends to keep husbands from entering more deeply into the emotional life of their wives? What are some practical ways husbands can live this out better? How can wives make it easier for their husbands to do this? And how can wives express their legitimate need for tenderness without falling into complaining or manipulating?

chapter eleven

How Contraception Harms Love

While many authors have written about the church's teaching on contraception, John Paul II goes a step further. He reflects not simply on why contraception is a moral issue, but even more, on how contraception actually can destroy the love between a husband and wife in marriage. Here, we will consider four points from his reflections on this topic.

ACCEPTING THE POSSIBILITY OF PARENTHOOD

First, John Paul II stresses that for sexual relations to become a true union of persons, it must be accompanied in the mind and will by the acceptance of the possibility of parenthood. Sexual union itself does not automatically bring about a true union of love. A wife, for example, may go through the act of *physical* intimacy without experiencing a deep *personal* intimacy with her husband—an intimacy based on her sense of his total love and commitment to her.

One of the key ingredients needed to make the bodily union between a man and woman an expression of an even deeper personal union of love is a willingness to accept the possibility that through the sexual act, "'I may become a father' or 'I may become a mother'" (227–228).

This openness to the possibility of parenthood is crucial if love is to mature in a marriage. In fact, approaching one's spouse with a genuine openness to the possibility of parenthood represents one of the most profound expressions of love and total acceptance of the other person in marriage. When a husband and wife are truly open to life in their marital relations, it is as if they are looking each other in the eye and saying, "I love you so much that I am even willing to embark on the adventure of parenthood with you! I entrust myself to you so much that I am willing to become a partner with you in serving any new life that may come from this act."

> A wife, for example, may go through the act of *physical* intimacy without experiencing a deep *personal* intimacy with her husband.

In this light, we can see how openness to life actually increases the love between spouses and can even represent one of the highest points of selflessness in a marriage. Not only do husband and wife merely stand face-to-face, enthralled with each other and enjoying the good of their own relationship, but they also stand shoulder to shoulder *looking outward together* at the potential new life that may come from their love.

Side by side, they stand committed not only to each other's own good, but also to working together to serve this potential new life. When this happens, "The relationship between husband and wife is not limited to themselves, but necessarily extends to the new person, which their union may (pro)create" (227).

Thus, when a husband and wife accept the possibility of becoming parents together, their own relationship is deeply enriched. No longer is the relationship just about *me* or even *us*— no longer is it closed in on ourselves, focused on my enjoyment or even our enjoyment in this act. But when we are open to life, the marital relationship becomes also about how we together might serve another life that God could entrust to us through this act.

REJECTING PARENTHOOD, REJECTING ONE'S SPOUSE

Second, John Paul II shows how contraceptive sex is not just a rejection of the possibility of parenthood, but in the end, a certain rejection of the other person. It prevents the physical union of marital intercourse from blossoming into a full personal union of love. He explains that when couples willfully reject the possibility of parenthood, "marital intercourse cannot be said to be a realization of the personal order. Instead of a truly personal union all that is left is a sexual association without the full value of a personal relationship" (228).

Ultimately, any sexual relationship that rejects the possibility of parenthood will be based on the sexual values of the other person—those aspects of the person that bring me physical or emotional pleasure—not on the value of the person as she is in herself.

And that's the great damage contraceptive sex inflicts upon a marriage. According to John Paul II, when spouses deliberately reject the possibility of parenthood through the means of artificial birth control, the fundamental character of their sexual relationship changes dramatically. Instead of being a union of persons, in which the spouses are at least open to expanding their love by becoming partners in parenthood together, contraceptive sex moves their marital relations in the direction of becoming merely a "bilateral" relationship of enjoyment, with no other purpose than to be used as a means to pleasure (228). Instead of being viewed as a cocreator of love, the spouse now is seen primarily as a partner in a pleasurable experience.

In the act of love, spouses should be directing their attention to the other person as a person. John Paul II says, "the will should be wholly concerned with that person's good, the heart filled with affirmation of that person's specific value" (234). When a man, however, rejects the possibility of becoming a parent with his wife in the marital act, the focus of his experience in sexual intercourse becomes centered on sexual pleasure. The value of the woman as a person and the opportunity for their marital bond to deepen fades into the background. It's as if the man is saying, "I want the sensual pleasure from this act, but I reject the possibility of your becoming a parent with me."

"It's as if the man is saying, 'I want the sensual pleasure from this act, but I reject the possibility of you becoming a parent with me.'"

> When a man and a woman who have marital intercourse decisively preclude the possibility of paternity and maternity, their intentions are thereby diverted from the person and directed to mere enjoyment: "the person as co-creator of love" disappears and there remains only the "partner in an erotic experience." Nothing could be more incompatible with the proper ends of the act of love (234).

That's why openness to life in the sexual act is "an indispensable condition of love" (236). As John Paul explains, "When the idea that 'I may become a father'/'I may become a mother' is totally rejected in the mind and will of husband and wife nothing is left of the marital relationship, objectively speaking, except mere sexual enjoyment. One person becomes an object of use for another person, which is incompatible with the personalistic norm" (239).

PERIODIC CONTINENCE

Third, while couples should never *reject* the possibility of parenthood in sexual intercourse, John Paul II teaches that they do not need to "positively desire to procreate on every occasion when they have intercourse" (233). Sexual intercourse is needed for the good of deepening the marital relationship, not just for procreation. He explains:

> Marital intercourse is in itself an interpersonal act, an act of betrothed love, so that the intentions and the attention of each partner must be fixed upon the other, upon his or her true good. They must not be concentrated on the possible consequences of the act, especially if that would mean a diversion of attention from the partner (233–234).

Thus, as a wise pastor, John Paul II explains how couples should be *open* to the possibility of new life coming from sexual relations, but that they do not have to enter sexual relations with the specific intention to have a child. He says it would be enough for couples to say, "in performing this act we know that we may become parents and we are willing for that to happen" (234). This sheds light on why even elderly and infertile couples continue to have intercourse. Since they themselves have done nothing to inhibit the possibility of conception, they can still remain at least *interiorly* open to new life if it should occur.[1]

Furthermore, couples may face certain situations in which they desire to avoid the conception of a child. In those cases, they may choose to abstain from having sexual relations, especially in those periods in which the woman is most likely to be fertile. John Paul calls this practice "periodic continence."

Today, many Catholics practice periodic continence using the highly effective method known as Natural Family Planning (NFP). By refraining from the sexual act in the fertile periods of a woman's cycle, couples may avoid conception without in any way distorting the fundamental meaning of marital relations. As the pope explains,

> A man and a woman moved by true concern for the good of their family and a mature sense of responsibility for the birth, maintenance and upbringing of their children, will then limit intercourse, and abstain from it in periods in which this might result in another pregnancy undesirable in the particular conditions of their married and family life (243).

STILL OPEN TO LIFE

Finally, while periodic abstinence is a viable option for Christian spouses, John Paul II explains that it is allowable "only with certain qualifications" (240).

He says the most important point to consider involves the couple's attitude toward procreation. Periodic continence may be used to help regulate conception, but it should not be used to avoid having a family. "We cannot therefore speak of continence as a virtue where the spouses take advantage of the periods of biological infertility exclusively for the purpose of avoiding parenthood altogether, and have intercourse only in those periods" (242).

The pope then points out that the good of the family should be weighed seriously before practicing periodic continence. He notes that giving children siblings can contribute in an important way to a child's education and upbringing, since brothers and sisters form a natural community that helps shape the child. In fact, in one intriguing statement, he seems to indicate that the ideal *minimum* number of children for a family is three. He says that for the child to be formed well,

> it is very important that this human being should not be alone, but surrounded by a natural community. We are sometimes told that it is easier to bring up several children together than an only child, and also that two children are not a community—they are two only children. It is the role of parents to direct their children's upbringing, but under their direction the children educate themselves, because they develop within the framework of a community of children, a collective of siblings. (242–243)

JUST 1.5 KIDS?

The pope certainly is *not* saying that parents who have only one or two children are not able to raise children effectively. But he does seem to suggest that having at least three children forms a more ideal environment for the children to be raised in a family. Why would he say that?

> "I entrust myself to you so much that I am willing to become a partner with you in serving any new life that may come from this act."

At first glance, this number seems somewhat arbitrary, and he doesn't give much of an explanation. In light of what he has said elsewhere about love, however, he might be in part drawing upon the theme of "the bond of a *common good*"—how love is meant to unite two persons around a common aim that they are striving toward together (28–29).

This is clearly the case in marriage, in which two spouses are united around the common good of deepening their own union and serving any children they may have. But it may also be the case with the children themselves as they have the opportunity to strive together toward the common good of serving other siblings in the family.

When my wife and I had our second child, for example, it was fascinating to see our firstborn grow in love for her younger brother. She wanted to make him smile. She wanted to feed him. She wanted to clothe him. As he grew older, it was a joy to watch his own love for his sister develop and to see them playing with each other, enjoying each other, and serving each other.

Something significant changed in their relationship, though, when our third child came along. Suddenly, their days were filled not simply with playing with each other. Now they were fascinated *together* with the new baby in the home. As sister and brother, they began to turn their attention not just toward themselves, but together, toward their new little sister.

Together they would sing songs to her. Together they wanted to feed her. Together they tried to make her laugh. The two older siblings were learning to become not just playmates who enjoyed each other's company, but partners in serving a new life outside of themselves—their new baby sister.

That could be one reason why the pope implies three is the ideal minimum number of children in a family: With at least three children, two or more can work together to serve another, and thus their opportunities to grow in love, friendship, and virtue *as a community* are deepened even more on a daily basis in the home.

THE BLESSING OF CHILDREN

In conclusion, John Paul II reminds us that if we are considering periodic continence, we must weigh not just our own financial security or our own comfort and lifestyle preferences when desiring to regulate conception. We must seriously weigh the blessing additional siblings can be for the well-being of our other children, for our family life as a whole, and even for all of society. John Paul II warns that parents who decide to limit the size of their family without considering these wider goods can cause serious harm to the family and society.

> Parents themselves must be careful, when they limit conception, not to harm their families or society at large, which has an interest of its own in the optimum size of the family. A determination on the part of husband and wife to have as few children as possible, to make their own lives easy, is bound to inflict moral damage both on their family and on society at large, which has an interest of its own in the optimum size of the family. (243)

Again, there certainly may be circumstances when regulating the number of children through periodic abstinence is necessary and indeed part of parental duty (243). But the intention to limit the number of conceptions should never be a renunciation of parenthood itself. "From the point of view of the family, *periodic continence as a method of regulating conception is permissible in so far as it does not conflict with a sincere disposition to procreate*" (243).

Therefore, in periodic continence, spouses should not be seeking to "avoid pregnancy at all costs" (243). On one hand, couples who are only having sexual intercourse during the times when the woman is not fertile should still approach the sexual act with a willingness to accept the possibility of becoming a mother or father, even if they do not desire a pregnancy and are practicing periodic continence in order to avoid a pregnancy.

On the other hand, in addition to keeping their individual sexual acts open to life, they should also have "a general disposition" toward becoming parents in the broader scope of their marriage as a whole, since siblings are a good for children, for the family, and for society as a whole (243).

For Further Reading
Love and Responsibility, pp. 211–244

For Discussion and Reflection

1. How is openness to the possibility of parenthood not only desirable, but necessary for deepening love in a marriage? How does this openness help break down egoism that can eventually destroy spousal love?

2. In 1952, C.S. Lewis wrote that the growing social acceptance of contraception in his time would lead to more problems in marriages and to greater sexual immorality in the world:

> Contraceptives have made sexual indulgence far less costly within marriage and far safer outside it than ever before, and public opinion is less hostile to illicit unions and even to perversion than it has been since Pagan times.[2]

This quote by Lewis, from 1952, seems almost prophetic in light of our culture's current situation. What does Lewis mean by this? What are some of the things in sexuality and marriage that once were viewed as harmful to society but now are socially accepted? In light of Lewis's comment, how might these be traced back to the acceptance of contraception?

3. Following the death of his young wife, author Sheldon Vanauken wrote *A Severe Mercy*, an account of their life together. Prior to a conversion to Christianity, the couple shared what he later referred to as "the pagan love," which was well-intentioned but inherently flawed in various respects. In describing their initial worldview, he wrote, "If children could be raised by a nanny, we sharing them for a few hours each day, or even if we were farmers, children might be a good. But in the pattern of modern life, where they became the centre for the woman, they were separating. We would not have children."[3] How might this quote reflect the typical mentality of our contemporary culture regarding children? How does this compare to John Paul II's vision for the family?

4. One of the great heroines of our time, Mother Teresa of Calcutta, once said, "The child is the beauty of God present in the world, the greatest gift to a family."[4] How can children be viewed less as a commodity for couples to enjoy, or even a "right," and more as an invaluable gift from God? Read Psalm 127:3–5 for further reflection.

5. How would you explain that practicing "periodic continence" as John Paul II describes is different from contraception? What is the distinction?

6. John Paul II says periodic continence is allowable "only with certain qualifications" (240). What are some of those qualifications that must be considered? Why?

chapter twelve

Foundations for the Theology of the Body

Today much excitement stirs around John Paul II's the Theology of the Body, the 129 catechetical addresses he gave from 1979 to 1984 that have revolutionized the way many people now teach about love, sexuality, and marriage.

Lay Catholics may respond initially with enthusiasm to what they've heard about the Theology of the Body, but many of those who actually dare to read these addresses quickly find themselves overwhelmed by the depth of John Paul II's philosophical, theological, and indeed mystical thought on this topic.

Having a grasp of John Paul II's earlier work *Love and Responsibility*, however, will help those interested to make more sense out of the Theology of the Body. Readers of *Men, Women, and the Mystery of Love*, familiar now with the basic concepts of *Love and Responsibility*, might want to investigate the pope's more famous later work. In this chapter, therefore, we will briefly look at some key points from the Theology of the Body that will make this monumental series of addresses a bit more digestible and practical for lay readers.

"THE LAW OF THE GIFT"

In an age when many individuals approach their relationships as ways of seeking their own pleasure, interests, or gain, John Paul

II constantly reminds us that such self-assertion is a dead end that will never lead to the love and happiness we long for. Human persons are made for self-*giving* love, not a self-*getting* love, and they will find fulfillment only when they give themselves in service to others.

This "law of the gift"[1] is written in every human heart. Near the beginning of the Theology of the Body, John Paul II alludes to how this law is based on man being made in the image of the Triune God (Genesis 1:26). Since God exists as a communion of three divine Persons giving themselves completely in love to each other, man and woman—created in the image of the Trinity—are not made to live as isolated individuals, each seeking their own pleasure and advantage from the other. Rather, man and woman are made to live in an intimate personal communion of self-giving love, mirroring the inner life of the Trinity.

In the end, human persons will find the happiness they long for when they learn to live like the Trinity, giving themselves in love to others.

ORIGINAL SOLITUDE

John Paul II then reflects on God's statement about Adam: "It is not good that the man should be alone" (Genesis 2:18).

At first glance, this statement seems odd. Adam is *not* alone. God has placed him in a garden with water, trees, and vegetation. He has even put Adam alongside other flesh and blood creatures, the animals. Even though there are many other animal creatures with bodies in the Garden of Eden, Adam is still in some sense described as being alone.

This tells us that there is something about Adam that is not found in other bodily creatures. By noticing how he is different from the animals, Adam comes to realize that he is more than a body, that he has a spiritual dimension. As a body-soul creature, Adam is unique. There is nothing else in creation like him.

This poses a problem. If Adam is made to live the "law of the gift"—to give himself in a mutual relationship of love—then Adam, at this stage, is in a certain sense incomplete. He is not able to live out the law of the gift, for there is no one else like him to give himself to as an equal partner. There is no other human person, no body-soul creature, like him. This is why God says, "It is not good that man should be alone."

> We can view sex as a way of deepening personal union with our spouse. Or we can approach sex merely as a physical act with someone who happens to gives us pleasure.

John Paul II explains that man only finds fulfillment when he lives in a relationship of mutual self-giving, living not for himself but for another person. "When God-Yahweh said, 'It is not good that man should be alone' (Gn 2:18) he affirmed that 'alone,' man does not completely realize this essence. He realizes it only by existing 'with someone'—and even more deeply and completely—by existing 'for someone'" (*TOB*, 60).

ORIGINAL UNITY

In response to Adam's solitude, the Lord creates another human person, Eve, to be his wife. "Then the man said, 'This at last is bone of my bones and flesh of my flesh'" (Genesis 2:23). John Paul II notes that this is the first time man manifests joy and exaltation. Before this moment, he had no reason for rejoicing, "owing to the lack of a being like himself" (*TOB*, 45). But now he finally has someone to give himself to in this unique way. In ecstatic response, he sighs, "At last!" for now he is able to live out the law of the gift and thus becomes who he was meant to be through his union with her.

Next, John Paul II reflects on how man and woman "become one flesh" (Genesis 2:24). He notes that this oneness in flesh does not refer merely to a bodily union, but points to a deeper spiritual union, a union of persons.

Recall that a human person is not just a body, but consists of body *and soul.* John Paul II expounds on how this union of body and soul in a person sheds light on human sexuality. The body has a language that is able to communicate something much more profound than information or ideas. What one does in his body reveals his very self, "the living soul" (*TOB*, 61). The body expresses the person and makes visible what is invisible, the spiritual dimension of man (*TOB*, 56, 76).

This has dramatic implications for understanding sexual intercourse. The marital act is not meant to be merely a physical union. It is meant to express an even deeper *personal* union. Since the body reveals the soul, when man and woman give their bodies to each other in marital intercourse, they give *themselves* to each other. Bodily union is meant to express a deeper spiritual union. The physical intimacy is meant to express an even more profound personal intimacy (*TOB*, 57).

John Paul II calls this unique language of the body "the nuptial meaning of the body." He says our bodies have a nuptial character in the sense that they have "the capacity of expressing love, that love in which the person becomes a gift and—by means of this gift—fulfills the meaning of his being and existence" (*TOB*, 63).

In this light, we can see that the body will be an important arena in which the drama of relationships between men and women will be played out, for better or for worse. We can approach the bodily union of sexual intercourse as a means to deepening personal communion in marriage. Or we can engage in sexual intercourse primarily with our own pleasure in mind and without any regard for the body's capacity to express self-giving love—in other words, without any regard for the nuptial meaning God has given to the body.

Put starkly: We can view sex as a way of deepening personal union with our spouse, giving ourselves completely and expressing total commitment to the beloved as a person and to what is best for our spouse. Or we can approach sex merely as a physical act with someone who happens to gives us pleasure—without any real commitment to that person's well-being. This denigration of sex, pervasive in our culture today, certainly is a far cry from the beautiful nuptial meaning God has given to the body.

Original Nakedness

What does it mean that Adam and Eve were "naked, and were not ashamed" (Genesis 2:25)? Shame involves fear of another person, the sense that we're not sure we can trust that person. We fear being used or being hurt, so we are afraid of being vulnerable in letting others see us as we really are.

Originally, Adam and Eve were not ashamed. They each had complete confidence, trust, and security in their relationship. Their bodily nakedness pointed to an even deeper *personal* "nakedness," in which they felt free to bare their souls completely to each other without any fear of being used, misunderstood, or let down. Adam and Eve understood "the nuptial meaning of the body"—not just the body at face value, but the body's capacity to express love and the communion of persons.

How were they able to have this ideal relationship? Imagine being in a relationship in which there was absolutely no selfishness.

You knew that your beloved was always seeking what was best for you and not just his own interests. He truly viewed you as a gift that was uniquely entrusted to him, and he took this role seriously with a profound sense of responsibility.

This is the kind of relationship Adam and Eve had in the garden. Before the Fall, sin had not yet entered the world, and human persons had self-mastery over their passions and appetites. Thus, with total purity of heart, they each were free from

> They felt free to bare their souls completely to each other without any fear of being used, misunderstood or let down.

selfish desires and approached each other with reverence.

John Paul II explains that Adam and Eve saw each other with a supernatural perspective—with "the vision of the Creator" (*TOB*, 57). In other words, they saw each other the way God himself saw them. Adam saw not just the beauty of Eve's body, but the whole truth of his beloved as a person. And just as God rejoiced in creating man and woman by saying, "It is good!" so Adam would have looked upon his wife with a profound sense of awe and wonder, seeing her as the daughter of God who had entrusted herself to him in marriage.

Likewise, Eve would have accepted Adam interiorly as a gift and responded to him with similar love and responsibility. "Seeing each other, as if through the mystery of creation, man and woman see each other even more fully and distinctly than through the sense of sight itself.... They see and know each other with all the peace of the interior gaze, which creates precisely the fullness of the intimacy of persons" (*TOB*, 57).

In this environment of complete mutual love and responsibility, personal intimacy could flourish. "The affirmation of the person is nothing but the acceptance of the gift, which...creates the communion of persons" (*TOB*, 65). Originally, therefore, man and woman did not experience the walls of shame in their rela-

Free from sin, they were free to love.

tionship. Free from sin, they were free to love. In a relationship of total reciprocal love, the walls of shame are not necessary. Indeed, as John Paul II explains, "immunity from shame" is "the result of love" (*TOB*, 67).

ORIGINAL SHAME

Once sin entered the world, however, men and women lost the self-mastery necessary to keep selfish desires from growing and poisoning relationships. Wounded by original sin, man finds that it is no longer easy for him to control his passions and appetites. No longer do men and women easily look upon their spouse with "the vision of the Creator" ("It is good!"). No longer do they easily see the other as a person entrusted to their care as a gift. Love is tainted now by the selfish desire to use the other.

Imagine the shock Adam must have experienced at that first moment in which he felt the effects of original sin in his life. John Paul II says it is as if Adam "felt that he had just stopped...being above the world of" the animals, which are driven by instinct and desires (*TOB*, 116). Almost like the animals, Adam now finds himself powerfully swayed by his desire to satisfy his sexual desires.

No longer mastering their passions, man and woman tend to approach each other with selfish and lustful hearts. That's why Adam and Eve instinctively conceal their sexuality from each other the moment sin and lust enter their lives (*TOB*, 117). They each no longer have total trust that the other is truly seeking what is best for them. Instinctively, they know that their beloved may use them. Thus, the biblical account of the Fall tells us that right after Adam and Eve sinned in the garden, they were naked and ashamed (see Genesis 3:7).

The introduction of sin shatters the original unity of man and woman and hinders personal intimacy, for now the defense mechanism of shame enters their relationship. "This shame took the place of the absolute trust connected with the previous state of original innocence in the mutual relationship between man and woman" (*TOB*, 120).

John Paul II explains that the original unity of Adam and Eve dissolved at the Fall because without the total mutual selfless love and trust, they no longer felt free to truly give themselves to each other:

> Having facilitated an extraordinary fullness in their mutual communication, the simplicity and purity of the original experience disappear.... [T]hat simple and direct communion with each other, connected with the original experience of reciprocal nakedness, disappeared. Almost unexpectedly, an insuperable threshold appeared in their consciousness. It limited the original giving of oneself to the other, in full confidence in what constituted their own identity. (*TOB*, 118)

BACK TO THE GARDEN?

As sinful creatures constantly battling concupiscence, we may never be able to return to the ideal relationship of pre-fallen Adam and Eve. However, there is hope. Through Christ's redemptive work in our lives, we may begin to experience the healing of those disordered passions that keep us from the great trust, love, and personal communion that God wants us to experience in our relationships.

The more the Holy Spirit transforms our selfish and lustful hearts with the total self-giving love of Jesus Christ, the more relationships between men and women will begin to recover something of the original unity of man and woman and the nuptial meaning of the body (*TOB*, 213).

FOR FURTHER READING
Theology of the Body, pp. 25–127

FOR DISCUSSION AND REFLECTION

1. What is the "law of the gift"?
2. Have you personally experienced the fulfillment that results from self-giving love? How did it change you?
3. Why was it not good for Adam to be alone? Was it simply because he was lonely? Explain.
4. Explain in your own words the "nuptial meaning of the body."
5. Matthew Kelly wrote:

> We can't be loved for who we are if we won't reveal ourselves. Unrevealed, we never experience intimacy. Unwilling to reveal ourselves, we remain always alone.... We hide because we think people will love us less if they truly know us, but the opposite is true in most cases. If we are willing to take the risk and reveal ourselves for who we are, we discover that most people are relieved to know that we are human.... Strong and weak, the human person is amazing. Our humanity is glorious and should be celebrated. When we reveal our struggles, we give others the courage to do the same.[2]

Before the Fall, Adam and Eve experienced "nakedness without shame": they felt free to bare their bodies and souls completely to each other because they had complete confidence, trust, and love in their relationship. Although sin entered the world, how is deep intimacy still possible through the redemptive love of Christ?

6. George Weigel wrote:

> What does all this business about love and Love come down to for you? Simply this: never settle for less than the spiritual and moral grandeur which, by grace, can be yours. They are your baptismal birthright as a Christian.
>
> You will fail. You will stumble on the ladder of love, and you will fall. That's no reason to lower the bar of expectation. That's a reason to get up, dust yourself off, seek forgiveness and reconciliation, and try again. If you settle for anything less than the greatness for which you were made—the greatness that became your destiny at baptism—you're cheating yourself. If you settle for anything less than the greatness that has been made possible for you by Christ, you're ignoring the twitch of the divine weaver on the thread of your life. Let His grace lift you up to where, in your heart of hearts, you want to be.[3]

How have the challenges presented by John Paul II in *Love and Responsibility* and the Theology of the Body given you inspiration and hope? How can you allow these truths, coupled with the transforming love of Jesus Christ, to continually alter the way you live your life?

7. What is the one truth in this study of *Love and Responsibility* that you found most life changing? How will you apply this insight to your life? How can you share it with others?

chapter thirteen

Single? Training for Marriage Right Now

You do not have to be engaged to start marriage prep. In fact, when speaking to young adults, I often remind them that they already are doing marriage preparation, even if they are not planning a wedding. For the way they live out their friendships, interact with the opposite sex, date, and live in community with others shapes the many habits they will bring into their marriages—for better or for worse.

It reminds me of how I once invited a semi-pro soccer player to run some practice sessions for my nine-year-old boys recreational team. As soon as he stepped on the field, I knew things were going to be different. He looked the players in the eye and said, "Boys, you'll play how you practice. If you practice well, you will play well. If you work hard at practice, you are going to work hard during the game. But if you don't give your best at practice, you won't give your best in the game. If you make mistakes in practice and don't correct them, you'll make mistakes in the game."

The boys responded to the challenge. They gave their all at every training session. They ran hard, worked hard, and fought hard in every drill, exercise, and scrimmage. And in just two seasons, our little mediocre band of boys turned into one of the top teams at the state tournament. The coach was right: "You'll play how you practice."

The same is true with marriage.

You want to use your single years as a time to practice—to fine tune the many virtues you will need to live out a strong marriage someday if, in fact, God leads you to that vocation. Here are a few things you can put into practice right now while single. These tips will not only help you get ready for marriage someday; they will also help you make a choice to live a certain way now so that you can make your life more of a gift to God and to others in whatever state of life you may find yourself.

1. BECOME A MAN OR WOMAN FOR OTHERS

Marriage will push you beyond what you could ever imagine in terms of generosity, love, and sacrifice. Suddenly, you will find yourself with another person and all of his or her needs, desires, expectations, and preferences, not to mention weaknesses, fears, hurts, and faults. And then, if you are blessed with children, you'll have little people who constantly need your care and attention, and you'll find less and less time for yourself. For many, the transition from singlehood to marriage and family life can be completely overwhelming. Marriage certainly comes with many thrills and joys, but also many unexpected challenges, trials, and crosses.

Why is marriage so demanding? I know a priest who, when preparing couples for marriage, says to them on the first day, "You might think you know what marriage is, but you don't. Here's the real definition of marriage: Marriage is never getting to do what you want!"

He says it with a smile, somewhat jokingly. But there is a truth here. We have seen how betrothed love entails a complete gift of one's self. And that requires a real dying to one's own interests, comforts, and preferences in order to serve one's beloved. Such sacrificial, self-giving love is hard for everyone. But it is especially challenging if during our singlehood we get too used to doing what we want all the time.

When we are single, dating, and engaged, we can, for the most part, live however we want. We can do what we want, spend our time how we want, spend our money how we want, hang out with our friends whenever we want. But in marriage, we are challenged to realize at a much deeper level how life is not all about *me*. We may know this as a single person, but we are confronted with this reality in a much more intense way when we enter marriage.

If we have devoted much of our single years, however, to pursuing our own interests, entertaining ourselves, avoiding conflict, and doing what we want all the time, it will not be easy for us to make sacrifices, to seek what is best for our spouse, to be patient with our beloved's shortcomings, or to wake up at 3 A.M. to take care of a crying baby.

> Every day God gives you many ways to get more outside of yourself and serve other people's needs.

But right now, whether you are single, dating, or engaged, you have dozens of opportunities to sharpen your sword and practice service to others. Every day God gives you many ways to get more outside of yourself and serve other people's needs. Apart from God's grace, nothing will prepare you more for the realities of marriage. In an era that tends to view the young adult years as a time for self-discovery and having fun, single people should be even more intentional about being *self-less*, about living to serve other people's needs and not just their own.

You can do this, for example, by fulfilling your commitments. When you say you are going to do something, follow through on it. Don't RSVP to an event and then fail to show up because something more interesting comes along. Your future spouse and kids need you to be someone they can depend on, a man or woman of your word.

You can also go out of your way to seek opportunities to serve. When you show up at a social gathering, are you the kind of person who looks around for what is most interesting, most pleasing, or most fun for you? Or are you the kind of person who walks into the room and thinks of how you can make the situation better for others? Your future spouse and children will need you not only to respond to their needs, but to be the kind of person who can anticipate how best to serve them.

Or when you have tension with a housemate or coworker, do you tend to evade the person, avoid the conflict, or pretend everything is OK out of fear? Or do you rise above your emotions and work through difficulties with the people in your life? Addressing conflict in a healthy way, rather than selfishly running away from it all the time, is an act of self-giving love. Learning this skill while single is one of the greatest gifts you can take into your future marriage.

2. LOOK FOR CHARACTER NOT CHARM

We might find ourselves very attracted to someone's good looks or taken in by their charming personality. But as we have seen throughout this book, real love requires a lot more than sensual attraction or powerful emotions. To love is to will the good of the other—to seek what is best for one's beloved. And if you want someone who will do a lot more than make you feel good in the present, someone who will truly love you for the long-term in marriage, you want to ask yourself some very important questions.

First, how does your beloved treat family and friends? That will reveal a lot about how he will treat you. Does he tend to be kind and honoring to his parents and siblings? Or is he disrespectful and complaining in his interactions with them? Does your beloved tend to put others' needs before her own interests, or is she more focused on herself? Would you describe her more as *self-less* or *self-centered*? How people interact with those closest to them says a lot about their character and their deep-rooted patterns of behavior. Your beloved's relational habits—whether they are full of generosity, humility, and self-control or selfishness, pride, and indulgence—are what he or she will bring into a future marriage with you.

Second, how virtuous is your beloved? We cannot expect our future spouse to be a saint right away. But we all, hopefully, are saints in the making. So we should ask the question of virtue: Does my beloved have the basic life-skills such as prudence, courage, self-control, kindness, and generosity to pour out his or her life completely for me and my future children? These basic life skills are the virtues. And the virtues matter so much more than the warm feelings we have when we are thinking about this person.

Whether your beloved looks good in a certain T-Shirt, is well-liked by everyone, or is really athletic does not matter as much as his ability to fight for you, protect you, and do all he can to set aside his own interests and serve you. Similarly, no matter how good-looking a girl may be and how much you like to hang out with her, if she does not have the ability to shoulder a lot of responsibility and consistently serve other people, she is not likely to be able to seek what's best for you, your marriage, and your family because she is too caught up in herself. People certainly can grow, and God's grace can help them overcome various weaknesses, but the question of virtue must be seriously weighed. That's what your beloved will bring into your marriage day-to-day—not the lovely wedding dress or handsome tuxedo, but character.

3. Don't Settle

Sometimes people are so desperate to be married—so afraid of being alone—that they settle for situations that are not likely to work well. There are several ways people do this. First, some move forward with marriage even if there are serious problems in the relationship. In their fear of never marrying, they make excuses for their beloved and try to convince themselves that the issues are not as bad as they think. They tell themselves, "Well, it could be a lot worse.... He's not an addict, and he's not abusive. He's really not that bad of a guy." Or, "Yes, I didn't like how she acted, but she has only done that a few times.... It probably won't be a problem once we're married." Or they secretly hope they can change their beloved once they are united in marriage. When people marry out of fear, they settle for someone whom deep down they know has significant problems. And once married, they usually regret that they ignored the warning signs.

> "You think it won't be a big deal, or you tell yourself, 'Maybe I can change him.' But the reality is you don't want to be married for forty years and lonely."

Second, other couples might have a good, healthy dating relationship, but they have different views of what they want for marriage and family life. One person wants to have a lot of kids, while the other is very afraid of having children. One person wants to stay at home while the other thinks it is important for both to have an income. One person wants to live near family, while the other wants to live wherever the best career opportunities come.

If the couple has strong divergent views on fundamental issues about their life together, the marriage is likely to face many additional challenges.

Third, one of the biggest trials in marriage can come when there are differences of faith. Marriages in which husband and wife have different faith perspectives can work. As the *Catechism* explains, "Difference of confession between the spouses does not constitute an insurmountable obstacle for marriage, when they succeed in placing in common what they have received from their respective communities..." (CCC 1634). But you should know the real crosses and challenges that come. "Differences about faith and the very notion of marriage, but also different religious mentalities, can become sources of tension in marriage, especially as regards the education of the children" (CCC 1634).

Sometimes the greatest trials in interfaith marriages are simply a lack of a deeper unity—a sense that something is missing, a sorrowful longing for something more. People who have a spouse of a different faith perspective often comment on how sad it is to be unable to share fully what matters most in life with the person they love. As one woman put it, "I love my husband. He is a very good man. We share a lot together. But I can't share what is dearest to me: my faith. When you're young, you think it won't be a big deal, or you tell yourself, 'Maybe I can change him.' But the reality is you don't want to be married for forty years and lonely."

4. Embrace the Wait

One of the greatest heartaches some single people experience is the uncertain waiting for a Mr. or Mrs. Right to come along. Some wonder why they have to wait so long. Others start to panic and fear that they will never get married. Many, unfortunately, focus only on the challenges and sufferings (however real they may be) and fail to see that God has a purpose for their life in this period. Indeed, the waiting itself is a part of the wonderful work God wants to do in their souls, if only they would meet him there.

If you are called to marriage but have not found your spouse yet, rejoice in this period as a time of special formation. We must have the confidence that all is in God's providence and that this time is a part of God's plan for you right now and for the blessings he wants to bestow on your future marriage. God may be doing many things in your soul at this moment. In your yearning for a spouse, for example, God may want to draw out an even deeper desire in your heart, which is for him alone. As much as you might long for a boyfriend or girlfriend or for a spouse who will love you totally, unconditionally, and for the rest of your life, no human person—not even the best of spouses—could ever fulfill your heart's deepest desires. Our hearts are restless, St. Augustine said, until they rest in God. Notice how he did not say our hearts are restless until they rest in the arms of a fiancé! The best of brides or grooms will still leave us thirsting for something more: the God who loves us. And God loves us too much to ever let us remain unclear about that fundamental truth.

But there may be other reasons why God has not yet brought you to your soulmate. Perhaps God wants you to use this time to grow more in virtue and service to others. Maybe he wants you to cling to him more in prayer so that you have an even stronger habit of prayer to bring to your married life. Or maybe there is some hurt from your past or some habitual sin or some dysfunctional pattern of relating to others that God wants to heal. Perhaps God may have you in the single state so that you can serve him in a unique way that would not be possible if you were in a serious relationship. We must also be open to the possibility that God is not calling us to marriage but to single life or a religious vocation. Whatever the case may be, the most important thing to do is trust that God does have a purpose and mission for you in this time of singlehood and to ask him what that might be.

In fact, God wants to meet you in your singlehood and invite you to experience his love and his power in your life right now. If we are only discouraged about our state in life and despairingly running away from it all the time, we may miss profound opportunities God is giving us to grow. God is real. He is present in your life. Do not resent the current situation or live in a fantasy about the future. Encounter him with you right now in the present.

FOR DISCUSSION AND REFLECTION

1. Does it really matter how we live our single years? In your own words, explain how our habits of relating to others right now—whether it be in our families, friendships, responsibilities, or dating relationships—will impact our future marriages?

2. In what ways are young people today tempted to live their single years more for themselves and not for others? If you could pick one thing to change or do in your life right now that would help you become more of "a man or woman for others," what would that be? How might that help prepare you for marriage and family life?

3. Why do you think some people settle for dating relationships and even marriages with people they know are not the best fit?

4. Our single years are not just a time of waiting for a spouse, but a time for formation. What do you think God wants to work on the most in *you* now before you get married?

chapter fourteen

For Engaged Couples:
Preparing Your Heart for Your Spouse

Nothing can ever fully prepare you for the mystery of your marriage. God is about to join you and your beloved in a most profound union that will bless you, stretch you, and shape you more than anything else in your life. Marriage classes and retreats can help cast a vision for the sacrament of matrimony. Good books and programs can help you work on communication, conflict, budgeting, and other practical life skills crucial for the married state. But the most important work God has in store for your marriage preparation will take place in your hearts.

Here are four key ways you and your fiancé can prepare your hearts to be joined together in marriage.

1. Turn Your Heart Outward toward Others: Real Love
We can sometimes have an overly romantic view of married love, as if it's about husband and wife staring into each other's eyes, holding hands, and sipping red wine together under the moonlight with an Italian love song playing quietly in the background.

But the realistic picture of married love is more like this: You are trying to eat your dinner with one hand while feeding a baby with the other. You want to talk to your spouse who is at the other end of the table, but other kids keep interrupting you with cries for more food, spilled drinks on the floor, complaints about how Bobby stole their favorite dinosaur that day, and questions about whether Johnny can come over next weekend. Amid the chaos, you finally make eye contact with your spouse as if to say, "Is this what we really signed up for when we got married?"

And the answer, of course, is yes. True love, as St. John Paul II taught, draws a man and woman beyond just their own love for each other and into a deeper love found in serving the children who embody their love. Real love is not about two people staring into each other's eyes and enjoying romantic feelings. Married love, especially when blessed with children, is more about husband and wife

> Amid the chaos, you finally make eye contact with your spouse as if to say, "Is this what we really signed up for when we got married?"

standing shoulder to shoulder and looking outward together: pouring their lives out together to serve the children God has entrusted to them. In this vocation, husband and wife will be stretched like never before. They will give up countless hours of sleep, leisure, free time, and financial resources. But in this outward-looking love, they each will find their own lives enriched and their union deepened in a way that no moonlight, red wine, or love song could ever accomplish. For in total self-giving love, they are living the way God made them, and it is only there that they will find their happiness.

To get ready for the reality of marriage and family life, one of the best things you can do is go out of your way to find opportunities to work together to serve others as a couple. Volunteer together at your parish. Help serve the poor together. Offer to babysit for families. In other words, do not just spend alone time together. Spend some time together *serving others* because that's what real marriage and family life is all about. Intentionally seek opportunities not just to gaze into each other's eyes, but also to stand shoulder to shoulder looking outward toward serving some good outside of yourselves—whether it be with your work, church, friends, or family.

2. Prepare Your Heart for Greater Self-Giving

Falling in love is easy. But growing in love is more difficult. The sparks of attraction, the rush of emotions, and the desire to be together all the time draw a couple closer initially. But such a love is not enough to sustain a relationship for long. That love must mature into something involving more of the will, not just the emotions. On your wedding day, the priest does not ask you, "Are you in love?" or "How do you feel about each other?" Rather, he asks about your will, your commitment, your ability to serve your beloved until death: "Have you come here freely and without reservation *to give yourselves to each other* in marriage? Will you love and honor each other as man and wife *for the rest of your lives?*"

A mature love is not a feeling, but a choice. It is centered on a will that has been trained to set aside one's own interests to serve what's best for the other. In engagement, the couple's love should become even more purified: more sacrificial, more focused on the other person, more of a committed choice to serve.

That's why we must prepare our hearts to go into marriage ready to change. When we are single, each individual can focus primarily on his own interests, plans, and desires. But marriage changes all that. It is no longer about what *he* wants or what *she* wants. It's more about a "we"—what is truly best for us as a married couple and what's best for our children.

Engagement gives couples the chance to practice that kind of selfless love in a deeper way. Whether it's supporting each other through the stresses and emotional roller coaster of planning a wedding, figuring out how you and your fiancé fit in with each other's families, or working through your first intense argument, engaged couples have many new opportunities to die to self.

As you prepare to make the total gift of yourself in marriage, your life—your time, your energy, your priorities—is now being claimed by someone else in a new way. This other person is definitively becoming the most important thing in your life next to God and needs your attention in a new way. Responding to the heightened needs of your beloved in engagement is crucial.

Moreover, the way you live all other areas of your life suddenly takes on new significance. How you approach your finances, how you manage any debt, how you take care of your health, how you daily work to advance your career—these are not issues that affect just you anymore. They greatly impact how you will be able to provide for your future marriage and children. Similarly, issues such as how you live your faith, how you guard your purity, how you handle stress and conflict, and how you interact with your future in-laws are not just matters of personal morality and spirituality, but shape the habits you will bring into your marriage and will greatly affect your future spouse and children. Engagement challenges us to live moment to moment more with the other person in mind, with a profound sense of responsibility for our beloved. Our life is not our own in marriage, and we begin living with that important truth in mind more pointedly during engagement.

3. Open Your Heart More to Your Beloved

Engagement also is an important time to get to know each other at a much deeper level—a time to be more vulnerable with each other. Hopefully, you have already cultivated a basic kind of trust in your relationship thus far. Now it's time to take that openness a step further.

When you are dating, you may start to picture a future life together with your beloved. You might wonder in your head, "*If I marry this person, maybe we'd live in that kind of a house, or maybe we'd have to move farther from my family, or maybe we'll have this amount of kids, or maybe we'd raise children in this way...*" But in dating, we usually do not talk about all these things just yet—at least not in depth. We are still holding back a bit, waiting for the full commitment of engagement. Once you are engaged, however, all that changes. All those "ifs" become "whens." All those possibilities become realities on the horizon. Important topics need to be discussed. Decisions need to be made.

"It's no longer about what he wants or what she wants. It's more about a 'we'—what is truly best for us as a married couple."

Now is the time to share more from your heart about your hopes for your life together. Have conversations about a whole array of crucial topics—faith, finances, work, sex, openness to having children, raising children, where to live, how to interact with extended family, where to celebrate holidays. Have frank discussions about the ways each of you were raised and how that might affect your relationship moving forward regarding things like approaches to conflict and expectations about money, cleanliness in the home, work, and family time.

Engaged couples also might open up more about their real fears, weaknesses, and struggles in life. They might be more open about mistakes and wounds from their past. All this is going to come out eventually. You can't hide your true self in your marriage. Engagement is a period when you can begin to unpack some of this.

In sum, think of this as a time to open more of your heart—your true self, as you really are, with all your dreams, hopes, insecurities, hurts, and shortcomings—so that you can give more of yourself to your fiancé. It is also a time to welcome your fiancé into your heart, as he or she really is, as a gift.

4. Turn Your Heart More toward God: Prayer

Archbishop Fulton Sheen once said it takes three to get married: husband, wife, and God. Indeed, it is God who joins the couple together in the sacrament of matrimony. But it's also God who continuously helps the couple grow in love and face the many challenges, trials, and sufferings that come up throughout their married lives.

> My wife needs a lot more than my love for her.... She needs Christ's love working through me.

Marriage is not something you can succeed in with your own abilities. You will find yourself pushed to whole new levels of generosity, patience, humility, and forgiveness as your weaknesses and faults rub against the weaknesses and faults of your spouse. You will often do selfish things that hurt your spouse. You will fail to express the honor and gratitude that you desire. And you will fail to love your beloved the way you really want. This is why we need God's grace to help us to love our spouse better than we could all on our own.

In my marriage, I know my wife needs a lot more than my love for her. My love is sincere and has some noble aspects, but it is tainted by much selfishness, pride, fear, and stubbornness. She needs not just my weak, fallen love, but Christ's love working through me, enabling me to love her much more than I would be able to do on my own. Similarly, my kids need a lot more than my own fallen love for them. They need Christ's love working through me so that they look up and see no longer me but Christ radiating through me.

This is the great blessing of the sacrament of matrimony. The sacrament is not just something to be celebrated on our wedding day. The sacrament forms a bond between husband and wife and a font of graces is made available to the couple throughout their married lives. We want to draw upon those graces regularly, begging God to help us love our spouse in the ways he or she needs to be loved each day. And as we draw upon the graces of the sacrament, we can say with St. Paul, "It is no longer I who live but Christ who lives in me."

But, for the graces of the sacrament to bear the most fruit in your life, you need to develop the habit of prayer right now during engagement. First, take time each day to pray, to have intimate conversation with God. Encountering the Lord daily in prayer is crucial for a strong marriage. In prayer, God invites us to love more in certain ways, and we experience his power to change our weak, selfish hearts. The more our hearts are transformed by Christ in prayer, the more we will love our spouse and children.

Second, pray together as a couple. Simply take some time each day to ask God to prepare your hearts for marriage, to give you each day your daily love, to help you to honor and serve each other moment to moment. Couples who come together to pray each day open their hearts to receive God's blessing and guidance in their lives.

Third, frequent the sacraments of the Eucharist and confession. By receiving Jesus in the Eucharist and regularly encountering his forgiveness and healing grace in the sacrament of reconciliation, our hearts are being shaped ever more by Christ's love. If you take these three simple steps—praying on your own, praying as a couple, and frequenting the sacraments—you will be cultivating the habits of prayer you will need to bring into your marriage. Your fiancé needs you to do this. Your future kids need you to do this. Do you want to give the best to your future spouse and children? Then give not just yourself, but God working through you in prayer. After all, it takes three to get married.

FOR DISCUSSION AND REFLECTION

1. In what ways is real married love not merely about "gazing into each other's eyes and enjoying romantic feelings" but about husband and wife "standing shoulder to shoulder looking outward"—outward toward serving some good outside of themselves? What are some things you and your fiancé can do now as a couple to prepare yourselves for this kind of love—a loving mission of serving others as a team in marriage and family life?

2. In this chapter, we saw how during engagement, "your life—your time, your energy, your priorities—is now being claimed by someone else in a new way." How have you noticed this reality in your relationship since you have been engaged? How have you responded to the new demands of your relationship and the needs of your beloved? Why is this so important for your future marriage?

3. Engagement is a time for couples to open their hearts to each other more. Are there any topics you have not felt comfortable discussing with your fiancé—whether about your personal past, your future together, faith, finances, or family life? What do you wish you knew more about in terms of what your

fiancé thinks? What do you wish you could share with your fiancé more from your own heart?

4. According to archbishop Fulton Sheen, a famous Catholic bishop from the twentieth century, it takes three to get married: husband, wife, and God. What did he mean by this? Why is a relationship with God in prayer so essential for a successful marriage? What can you do now to deepen a daily prayer life—individually and as a couple? How will this habit of prayer help you in your marriage?

CHAPTER ONE: *The Three Kinds of Friendship*

1. Janet Smith, "John Paul II and *Humanae Vitae*," in *Why Humanae Vitae Was Right* (San Francisco: Ignatius, 1993), p. 232.

2. For a more extensive treatment of friendship in Aristotle, see John Cuddeback, *Friendship: The Art of Happiness* (Greeley, Colo.: Epic, 2003).

CHAPTER THREE: *Avoiding Fatal Attractions*

1. The pope specifically discusses this topic of art and pornography later in *Love and Responsibility*. First, he says that art may at times portray the sexual aspect of man and woman and their love for each other.

> Art has a right and a duty, for the sake of realism, to reproduce the human body, and the love of man and woman, as they are in reality, to speak the whole truth about them. The human body is an authentic part of the truth about man, just as its sensual and sexual aspects are an authentic part of the truth about human love. (192)

The pope goes on to say, however, that it would be wrong to portray the *sexual* values in a way that overshadows the true *value of the person*. And it would be wrong to portray the sexual aspect of a couple's relationship in a way that obscures their authentic love for each other, which is much more than sexual. This is the problem with pornography: It draws attention to the sexual aspect of a man or woman in a way that prevents us from seeing the true value of the person and the full truth of love.

Pornography is a marked tendency to accentuate the sexual element when reproducing the human body or human love in a work of art, with the object of inducing the reader or viewer to believe that sexual values are the only real values of the person, and that love is nothing more than the experience, individual or shared, of those values alone. This tendency is harmful, for it destroys the integral image of that important fragment of human reality which is love between man and woman. For the truth about human love consists always in reproducing the interpersonal relationship, however large sexual values may loom in that relationship. Just as the truth about man is that he is a person, however conspicuous sexual values are in his or her physical appearance. (192–193)

2. C.S. Lewis, *A Mind Awake: An Anthology of C.S. Lewis*, Clyde S. Kilby, ed. (New York: Harcourt, 1968), pp. 192–193.

CHAPTER FOUR: *Sense and Sentimentality: The Proper Role of the Emotions*

1. C.S. Lewis, *Mere Christianity* (San Francisco: Harper, 1980), pp. 108–109.

2. John Paul II, Apostolic Letter on the Dignity and Vocation of Women (*Mulieris Dignitatem*) (Boston: Pauline, 1988), p. 19.

CHAPTER FIVE: *The Law of the Gift: Understanding the Two Sides of Love*

1. See Vatican II, *Gaudium et Spes* (The Church in the Modern World), 24.

2. Matthew Kelly, *The Seven Levels of Intimacy: The Art of Loving and the Joy of Being Loved* (New York: Simon and Schuster, 2005), p. 62.

CHAPTER SIX: *Love and Responsibility? Building Trust, Intimacy, and a Mature Love*

1. James Dobson, *Life on the Edge* (Dallas: Word, 1995), p. 94.
2. See John Paul II, *The Theology of the Body: Human Love in the Divine Plan* (Boston: Pauline, 1997), especially pp. 54–72.
3. John Paul II, *Ecclesia de Eucharistia* (Vatican City: Libreria Editrice Vaticana, 2003), 22.
4. Alice von Hildebrand, "Love, Marriage and Faithfulness in Søren Kierkegaard," *Philosophy Readings Manual*, Dr. Michael Healy, ed. (Steubenville, Ohio: Franciscan University Press, 1974), pp. 88, 97, 104.
5. Søren Kierkegaard, *Works of Love*, Edward and Edna Hong, trans. (New York: Harper, 1962), pp. 168–169.

CHAPTER EIGHT: *The Battle for Purity*

1. Francis De Sales, *Introduction to the Devout Life*, John K. Ryan, trans. (New York: Doubleday, 1996), p. 148.

CHAPTER NINE: *To Inspire Love: A Return to Modesty*

1. Wendy Shalit, *A Return to Modesty: Discovering the Lost Virtue* (New York: The Free Press, 1999), p. 72.

CHAPTER TEN: *Men, Women, and Tenderness*

1. Karol Wojtyla, *The Jeweler's Shop* (San Francisco: Ignatius, 1992), pp. 48–49, 51–52.

CHAPTER ELEVEN: *How Contraception Harms Love*

1. Couples "may continue to have sexual relations even in spite of permanent or temporary infertility. For infertility in itself is not incompatible with inner willingness to accept conception, should it occur. It makes no difference that conception may not occur because it is precluded by nature" (236).

2. C.S. Lewis, *Mere Christianity* (San Francisco: Harper SanFrancisco, 1980), p. 97.

3. Sheldon Vanauken, *A Severe Mercy* (San Francisco: HarperSanFrancisco, 1980), p. 37.

4. Susan Conroy, *Mother Teresa's Lessons of Love and Secrets of Sanctity* (Huntington, Ind.: Our Sunday Visitor, 2003), p. 153.

CHAPTER TWELVE: *Foundations for the Theology of the Body*

1. Catholic commentator George Weigel calls this "the law of the gift." See, for example, G. Weigel, *Witness to Hope* (New York: HarperCollins, 1999), p. 136.

2. Matthew Kelly, *The Seven Levels of Intimacy: The Art of Loving and the Joy of Being Loved* (New York: Simon and Schuster, 2005), p. 14.

3. George Weigel, *Letters to a Young Catholic* (New York: Basic, 2004), pp. 119–120.

ABOUT THE AUTHOR

Dr. Edward Sri is a theologian, author and well-known Catholic speaker. He has written several Catholic bestselling books, including *The New Rosary in Scripture* and *A Biblical Walk through the Mass*, which was used in about one out of four parishes in the USA in preparation for the new translation of the Mass. He currently serves as professor of theology and vice president of mission at the Augustine Institute in Denver, Colorado.

Dr. Sri is a founding leader with Curtis Martin of FOCUS (Fellowship of Catholic University Students). He is the host of the Augustine Institute's acclaimed twenty-part video series on the Catholic faith called *Symbolon: The Catholic Faith Explained* being used in thousands of parishes around the world for adult faith formation, RCIA, catechist formation, and family ministry. He also is the content director for the Institute's marriage preparation and marriage enrichment program called *Beloved: Finding Happiness in Marriage*.

His most recent books include: *Pope Francis and the Joy of the Gospel: Rediscovering the Heart of a Disciple*; *Walking with Mary: A Biblical Journey from Nazareth to the Cross*; and a video-based Bible study program on the Mother of Jesus called *Mary: A Biblical Walk with the Blessed Mother*.

Dr. Sri leads pilgrimages to Rome and the Holy Land. He regularly speaks at Catholic parishes, conferences, clergy retreats and diocesan catechetical congresses and is a frequent guest on Catholic radio and EWTN. He holds a doctorate from the Pontifical University of St. Thomas Aquinas in Rome and resides with his wife, Elizabeth, and their seven children in Littleton, Colorado.